THE FISHES OF THE SEA

Commercial and Sport Fishing in New England

THE FISHES OF THE SEA

Commercial and Sport Fishing in New England

Dave Preble

S

Sheridan House

First published 2001 by
Sheridan House Inc.
145 Palisade Street
Dobbs Ferry, NY 10522

Library of Congress Cataloging-in-Publication Data

Preble, Dave
    The fishes of the sea: commercial and sport fishing
  in New England/Dave Preble.
        p. cm.
    Includes bibliographical references
    ISBN 1-57409-132-8 (alk. paper)
        1. Fisheries—New England. 2. Fishing—New England.
    I. Title.

SH221.5.N4P74 2001
338.3'727'0974—dc21   2001049067

Designed by Jesse Sanchez

Printed in the United States of America

ISBN   1-57409-132-8

To the past, Capt. Burt Preble, Capt. Bob Linton, Capt. Al Sanchez, and all the other old-timers from whom I learned so much more than how to fish.

To the future, Katie, Logan, Laura, and Alison, children of a new age. May they have the wisdom to learn from our mistakes and the strength to stay free.

Be fruitful, and multiply, and replenish the earth, and subdue it; and have dominion over the fishes of the sea and over the birds of the heavens, and over every living thing that moveth upon the earth."
—*Genesis 1:28*

"And the fear of you and the dread of you shall be upon . . . all the fishes of the sea, into your hand are they delivered."
—*Genesis 9:2*

"Aye, them was the days, Davy, them was the days.
I saw the best of it. And you saw the last of it."
—*Capt. Bob Linton, the MAKO II*

Acknowledgments

During the writing, rewriting, and editing of this book, I came to appreciate Cervantes' observation that a writer is the child of his works. The writer may look to an audience, but the act of writing is personal and reflects the author's point of view at the time the words are set down. When the writing is polemical, as is much of this work, and engages a broad topic, the author's point of view is bound to be somewhat parochial and limited by his own experience. I have tried to use my experiences to honestly describe the effect of our often poor decisions on some of the people who live with those decisions.

Many people over many years have had a part in shaping this book. But in actually writing and producing it, two stand out. My wife, Meredith, kept my life together during the months of writing, and critiqued each day's output, a thankless task if ever there was one. Lothar Simon, of Sheridan House, turned an editor's cold gaze upon the final product and significantly strengthened it by forcing me to confront the parts that were written in anger, an emotion that leads to excessively florid prose, fractured syntax, and simple error.

Finally, I would like to thank Capt. Richard Allen, a commercial fisherman and among the industry's most articulate and informed spokesmen. Dick's conclusions often differ from mine, but his patient humor and prodigious knowledge have kept me from excessive self-assurance. When I rail on about destructive modern gear types, he quietly interjects the story of the decimation of the Atlantic halibut a century ago by primitive means and, thereby, reminds me that the problem is, ultimately, one of motive more than method.

CONTENTS

THE FISHES OF THE SEA

Commercial and Sport Fishing in New England

INTRODUCTION

The Genesis of New England's Continental Shelf and Its Living Resources

. . . time and chance happeneth to them all. For man also knoweth not his time.
—Ecclesiastes 9:11–12

Time is but the stream I go a-fishing in.
—Henry David Thoreau, *Walden*, 1854

Long before man appeared on this planet, three times farther back in time than the appearance of the first dinosaur, back when the first cells were joining in symbiosis to form the earliest multicelled organisms, the eastern coasts of the Americas were joined to the western coasts of Europe and Africa. Together they formed an enormous continent now known as Pangaea, and the Atlantic Ocean did not yet exist.

What would become, eons later, the northeastern United States was a land of high mountains with river-cut intermontane valleys, a land far from any sea. As millions upon millions of years passed, the mountains wore away under the steady movement of water from the clouds to the high ground to the rivers to the valleys. Into the valleys piles upon piles of sediments were layered down from the eroding mountains. The weight of these ever-increasing sediments stressed, twisted, and cracked the underlying mantle, and fiery molten granite forced its way up through the cracks. Much of the land subsided as the mountains eroded away, and in these lower areas swamps formed with junglelike forests in which dead plant material fell to the ground and piled up, year by year, over the ages compressing under its own weight and forming seams of coal.

Through all of the ages of the Paleozoic, in seas far away from the future Atlantic, soft multicelled life evolved into all of the major marine phyla that we know today: the sponges; the jellyfish and sea anemones; the bryozoans and brachiopods; the flatworms, roundworms, and segmented worms; the starfishes and sea urchins; the mollusks, octopuses, and squids; the trilobites, crabs, and lobsters; and all the families of fishes.

By the time of the very earliest dinosaurs the ancient mountains were gone, but a new disturbance, called the Appalachian orogeny, thrust up new mountains along the entire eastern portion of North America as the continent itself broke away from Europe and began to wander westward, the space in between gradually widening and forming the Atlantic Ocean. The level of the earth's waters rose and fell by hundreds of feet, time after time, as the continents separated and the ocean between widened and grew deeper. The dinosaurs flourished for more than 150 million years and then died out, and still the Atlantic grew wider. The floor of the ocean stretched and then split down its middle from the Arctic to the Antarctic, and molten rock from the earth's center poured out through the crack, solidified, and formed the longest mountain range on the planet—all under water. Finally, the mammals had their turn, evolving on land but some returning to the mother ocean in the form of whales, seals, dolphins, and porpoises.

The land of the northeast coast of America was formed in fire, but its final sculpting was done by ice. With fluctuations of the earth's heat balance, there came times when the snows of the Arctic winters did not all melt in the summer. As they piled up, the snows compressed under their own weight into sheets of ice as high as the top of present-day Mount Washington. Deepening and pushing ever southward, the ice locked up so much of the earth's water that the level of the ocean's surface fell several hundred feet, and dry land was exposed as far as one hundred miles out from the present shoreline. At least four times in the past 1.6 million years the great glaciers expanded south across New England and the upper Midwest and then receded as the earth once again warmed up.

Each time, the slowly creeping ice, unimaginable tons of it, scraped the earth clean. Its leading edge pushed a wall of rubble, fine gravel to ship-sized boulders, ahead of it. When the glaciers slowed, stopped, and finally receded, this terminal moraine of debris was left in a long line. Although much eroded, parts of one such moraine are still visible today as lines of islands south of New England, starting with the southern "fin" of Long Island to the west and including Block Island, Martha's Vineyard, and Nantucket Island to the east. The lower parts of the moraine are now underwater reefs and ledges, between and beyond the islands. These include the Southwest Ledge between Montauk Point and Block Island, the East Ground, Cox Ledge and the nineteen-fathom bank between Block Island and Martha's Vineyard, and Georges Bank, east of Nantucket.

The last glacier receded several miles, stopped, and deposited another moraine. This more inshore line of rubble now forms the northern "fin" of Long Island eastward to Orient Point, Fishers Island off Watch Hill on the Rhode Island coast, Browns Ledge, Sow and Pigs Reef, the boulder-strewn Elizabeth Islands, and part of the inner portion of Cape Cod.

Water streaming down from the melting glacier formed great rivers that cut valleys through the outer moraine and the land beyond. All the way to the still-dry edge of the continental shelf the rivers ran, then over the outer cliff in great canyon-cutting cascades to the ocean, several hundred feet below its present level. The glacial meltwater slowly refilled the ocean, and it returned to cover the continental shelf—drowning the canyons, drowning the valleys and plains, drowning much of the outer terminal moraine, leaving only islands where the deposits were highest.

It is not known when man first gazed out onto the Atlantic Ocean, and it is still easy to start an argument over who first crossed it. Cultural clashes and natural disasters have erased much of the history of our species, leaving just enough threads to tantalize anthropologists and historians. Genealogy may tell a story, but at best it is a short story, beyond which lies only speculation on just where one's personal threads may lead.

My own threads are first picked up for certain in the Scottish highlands—land of violent past, cult of cold steel, and bloody ground of Culloden Moor. In the terrible times of that battle my forebears left their home, crossed the stormy North Atlantic, and landed on the coast of Maine. They were hardly the first. By the time of their arrival in the mid-1700s Portland (then called Falmouth) was already a thriving seaport, and the British colonies to the south had been in existence for more than a century. Portuguese, French, and Spanish fishermen had been making the crossing for at least two centuries, and the Norsemen had built a town in Newfoundland five centuries before that. It is even possible that Irish monks crossed the Atlantic Ocean a full thousand years before the first of my ancestors left the Scottish highlands. Yet even the earliest Europeans on these shores found a native population that had migrated far earlier and from the other direction, crossing from Asia on dry land before the final melting of the last great glacier.

What they all found here was a land of enormous variety. The climate was temperate with four clearly defined seasons, and the soil was better than what most had left behind. There were inland mountain ranges grading to wide coastal plains, all covered by forests of white pine, hemlock, spruce, and mixed hardwoods. There were rivers from the mountains to the sea and a rocky coast interspersed with long barrier beaches that protected both brackish ponds and miles upon miles of salt marshes where fish and shellfish by the teeming billions were spawned. And the reefs and banks of the wide continental shelf held more fish than anyone had ever seen before.

CHAPTER 1

Groundfish; The JOHN AND JENNIFER, Part I;
Legislative Impacts; The JOHN AND JENNIFER, Part II

Perhaps the stocks of fish off New England might be so
well protected in the future that they will rebuild. Perhaps the
United States may even decide to renovate and upgrade its
New England fishing fleet to the level where it might be able
to supply a greater share of our demand for fish protein.
However, it seems increasingly unlikely that the
New England fisherman, as we now know him,
will long remain on the scene.
—David Boeri and James Gibson, *Tell It Good-Bye, Kiddo,* 1976

Are you sure this loan is big enough? Getting through the first
year can be tough, you know.
—A bank vice-president at the closing of a
federally guaranteed boat loan, 1984

The bottom of the ocean, at least out to the edge of the continental shelf, is referred to as "the ground." By extension,
the absolute speed of a boat is called speed over the
ground, as opposed to speed through the water, which may be different from absolute speed due to wind and current; the towing
line of a trawl that attaches the net to the spreading doors and

7

drags across the bottom is called the ground cable; an anchor with its chain and shackles is called ground tackle; a vessel that fetches up on the bottom is said to have run aground; and commercially important fish that inhabit the bottom are called groundfish.

All bottom fish, whether or not of commercial importance, are called *demersal finfish,* or just demersals. In contrast, the fish that spend most of their time away from the bottom, roaming the ocean (such as mackerel, tuna, and billfish), are called *pelagic finfish,* or just pelagics. These terms are not strictly exact, since pelagics may spend time on or near the bottom and demersals may move away from the bottom sometimes to feed.

The demersals tend to be slower swimmers than the pelagics, but they are better at maneuvering. They don't have the long migrations of most pelagics, so their muscle metabolism is different. For this reason their meat is whiter and less bloody and tends to have a longer shelf life. The traditional commercial fisheries in New England were mostly for demersals such as cod, haddock, pollock, hake, whiting, halibut, various flatfishes, and a couple dozen other species of lesser importance. New England charterboats, which take people out for a fee to fish with hook and line using a rod and reel, also target demersal species, chiefly cod, pollock, flounder, tautog, and scup (porgies).

The Atlantic cod, *Gadus morhua,* is the perfect demersal finfish for a charterboat. Cod breed profusely and feed on just about anything. They are easy to catch, and the firm white flesh is delicious, stores well, and adapts to many different ways of cooking. Cod prefer the type of rocky, gravelly bottom that the glaciers deposited on most of New England's continental shelf, but in times of abundance they can even be found on mud bottom or off sandy beaches. Cod are somewhat migratory, but fishermen who know where to look can find them within range in any month of the year—or at least they could before the populations crashed in the early 1990s.

Charterboats and head boats (charterboats "charter" the

whole boat to a group for a single rate; head boats take individuals as they come, "by the head") have been taking people codfishing on the U.S. East Coast since at least the very early twentieth century. Exactly how much earlier this practice began is difficult to determine; it is known that working lobstermen and tub trawlers of the previous century would at times hire out to take people fishing with rod and reel or handline, and paintings from the mid-nineteenth century show pleasure boats, some of which were surely for hire, handlining while at anchor or trolling fishing lines as they sailed. In 1870, John H. Rice, a forty-seven-year-old Narragansett Bay "fisherman by occupation," testified before a special fisheries committee of the General Assembly of Rhode Island that all the fishermen he knew would "carry out parties to fish" to supplement their incomes and that he had been doing so for twenty-four years.

Cod are among the most important of commercial fish and have been for generations. Portuguese fishermen were crossing the Atlantic to fish for cod on the Grand Banks south of Newfoundland more than a century before the Pilgrims made their crossing. The export of dried salt cod became so important to the economy of the Massachusetts Bay Colony that a huge wooden "sacred cod" was placed in the assembly chamber in Boston (where it still hangs). In the years before the Revolutionary War the cod became one of the mainstays of what historian Samuel Eliot Morison called "the wealth of the New World."

Codfishing was done in the early days by hook either at the end of a lead-weighted handline or as part of a long tub trawl line with many hooks on side lines (called snoods), the whole affair being wrapped up in a tub (hence the name). These centuries-old techniques were still the primary methods used when my grandfather was a young man, and to some extent they are still in use today. Around the beginning of the twentieth century the development of the internal combustion engine and its adaptation to use on fishing boats made towing a net possible, and by the time my father began commercial fishing in the 1930s, the towed otter trawl was in general use for catching demersal fish. This complicated device consists of a wide, low net whose mouth is held open by the water pressure against iron or wood-and-iron "doors" that are dragged along the bottom at an angle on each side of the net, and the trawlers that use them are called draggers.

The early draggermen worked hard and caught as much as they could in those days of no regulation yet didn't do much harm to the resource because their nets were fragile and the low power of their engines kept them small. After World War II there was a destructive offshore groundfishery by enormous foreign factory trawlers, which was described in the appropriately named book *Tell It Good-Bye, Kiddo* published in 1976, but it had little impact on the inshore groundfishery. Until around 1970 a charterboat could leave Point Judith, Rhode Island, at six o'clock in the morning, fish the rock piles east of Block Island or on Cox Ledge, and on most days return with a thousand pounds of cod by three o'clock in the afternoon. Many of the fish would weigh over forty pounds. A good single commercial handliner could figure on six hundred pounds of cod per tide during the spring and autumn runs. Even in the best of the "good old days" it really wasn't any better than that.

Then came the 1970s and three developments that altered the entire population structure of the demersal finfishes and threatened the future of all groundfisheries. The first of these developments was the high-output small diesel engine. The average dragger became larger, wider, and much more powerful. Nets became much larger and able to fish on more broken bottom, and their doors were moved far from the wing ends of the net by long ground cables that tore up the bottom and herded fish to the net's mouth. The second development, an offshoot of military and space technology, was inexpensive, precise navigation and fishfinding electronics. Not only could fishermen "see" the fish, but they could make tight sweeps, back and forth across the bottom the way a room is swept, and they could work very close to obstructions without fear of damaging the net. The third development was the production of nylon monofilament and the monofilament gillnet. Gillnets, which sit on the bottom and trap fish moving through the water, were nothing new, but they had always been too heavy and unwieldy to be of much practical use in the ocean. Making them of light monofilament line made it possible for very small boats to carry and easily deploy several, covering thousands of feet of bottom.

One impact of these changes was to eliminate all sanctuary areas for the fish. Although the old-timers caught all the fish they were able to, their methods couldn't be used on large areas of the bottom—areas that became de facto sanctuaries where fish bred and fed undisturbed. These sanctuaries would constantly replenish the grounds that the earlier gear could work. Today, if the bottom is too rough for a regular net, a fisherman can install a ground cable with "rockhoppers" and adjust the net to "fly." If it is too rough for that device or there is a submerged wreck or other large bottom obstruction, he can drop a gillnet on it. The newest wrinkle is the pair trawl, an enormous net towed between two very powerful boats that can be adjusted to fish any portion of the water column from the surface to the bottom. One major reason why the groundfisheries are in such deep trouble today is the loss of sanctuary. As Joe Louis used to say, "They can run, but they can't hide."

• • •

"Bring the doors aboard and batten down the trawl!" Jack yelled from the after pilothouse window. "God, what a beautiful night!" Jack felt good, and so did everyone else on the JOHN AND JENNIFER. We had a hell of a catch. Six-minute tows with an eight-minute turnaround time, eight tows in two hours through stacks of clear butterfish, and we had ninety thousand pounds aboard. A contract price from the Japanese of thirty-two cents a pound meant no haggling with buyers and a crew share of about twenty-four hundred dollars per man. Twelve hours steaming time each way and another eight hours for the lumpers to take out the fish still turned out to be damned good money, any way you looked at it.

We hoisted the doors into the boat and wound the last of the net onto the drum and secured it. Jack headed the boat north and set the autopilot. Then he turned and leaned out of the after pilothouse window again, his elbows on the sill, watching us work to sort the last two tows, almost twenty thousand pounds still on the deck, and push them through the deckhatches into the two forward pens while the holdman below iced them down as they fell through. Twice the holdman yelled up, "Hey, will you assholes slow down? I can't throw ice that fast!" The second time, one of the deckhands leaned into the deckhatch and hummed a fish at his head. Jack laughed and said to me, "Dave, why don't you go get supper going. These fellers can finish up on deck." As the last man hired, one of my functions was to cook.

The JOHN AND JENNIFER was designed to be run five-handed. Everyone worked on deck while we were actually fishing, but each man had another major duty. Jack was the captain and carried the responsibility for the boat and its crew. He decided where and for what we would fish, supervised the crew, and negotiated all fish sales. Joe Mendes, a Portuguese whose family had fished for generations, was the mate. He coordinated the crew on deck and directed the constant repairs and maintenance. If Jack were disabled, he would assume command. Dave Barker was the engineer. He maintained the main engine and transmission, the generator, and all the pumps and winches. To avoid confusion while working on deck, he was called Dave One and I was called Dave Two. Jimmy Lang was the holdman, a job I never envied. He would chop ice and shovel it in with the fish as they cascaded down through the deckhatches into the fish-pens. Each of the twelve pens held from five to seven thousand pounds of fish, and ice had to be evenly spread throughout them or hot spots of fermentation would begin and ruin the whole penful. My job was to cook and keep the boat provisioned with the enormous quantities of mostly high-calorie food that a fisherman on the North Atlantic consumes.

Once inside, I peeled out of my oilers and my Norwegian sweater and rolled up my sleeves. I peeled and boiled ten pounds of potatoes, stuffed and baked a dozen and a half slammer pork chops, cooked three pounds of frozen vegetables, and made a big salad. The freezer was loaded with ice cream, and we had cases of canned fruit and puddings. If nothing else, we surely ate well.

I was mashing the potatoes when the rest of the crew came in, still laughing over some incident of ballbusting on deck. Everyone was ruddy-faced from the wind and the cold and euphoric at the end of a good trip. The deckhouse was warm now, so everyone peeled down to his longjohns. Dave Barker went down through the forward companionway to check the gauges on the generator and grease the pumps. Joe turned on the VCR and put in a blue movie, real hard-core stuff. The movies were part of a ritual that didn't change from trip to trip. We would rent a half-dozen for each trip, but only one would be pornographic and that one would only be put on at the end of the trip. One other would be a "serious" film for the ride out when everyone was fresh, and the others would be B-grade action flicks that would be run for the three to thirty minutes between tows when we might be numb with fatigue. Dave Barker's wife once told me how much she hated us watching the porno, so I told her about monotony and sensory deprivation of being on the cold, gray sea and how at the end of the trip the stimulation served to reawaken our senses so that we could rapidly adjust to the far different environment of land and its people. Dave was shaking his head and trying not to laugh, but we were drinking and she looked serious and didn't seem to recognize the chicanery. "You know, I never thought of it that way," she said.

The three of us in the galley piled food on our plates and sat at the table, shoveling it in and watching the porno. Dave came back up from the engine room and joined us. "What's this one about?" he asked. "What are they all about?" Joe answered, his eyes not leaving the screen.

Jack came down from the pilothouse, singing loudly and slightly off tune, "Hey, diddly dee, a fisherman's life for me!" He filled a plate and said, "Hey, you did pretty good tonight, only one real fuck-up. How come you can't keep the winches running together?"

"Second wire marker's worn on the port side," Joe said. "Can't always see it."

"Well, you got to tell me these things. Next trip we'll change all the markers when we make our first tow. Now, what do you guys want to do about Christmas and New Year's?"

I said, "If I'm not home for Christmas I'll be spending the next two years paying for another divorce."

"All right, we'll plan on being in by the night of the twenty-third. What about New Year's?"

"Screw New Year's," Joe said. "The fishing's good, and that's just amateur night anyway!"

"All agreed?" Heads nodded. "Good! Dave, when you get done take the first wheel watch." The cook always took the first watch, but Jack liked to give the command. He returned to the pilothouse, still singing.

When the galley work was finished I poured a cup of coffee and went up to the pilothouse. The rest of the crew had headed for their bunks. Jack went below to get himself a cup of coffee too while I checked the course and the Loran, logged in our position on the chart overlay and initialed it. Then I checked the alarms, reset the autopilot, and went down to check the water level in the bilges. When I returned Jack was sitting at the chart table. I checked three sweeps in the radar at three-mile range, repeated it at twenty-four miles, and then visually scanned the ocean for other vessels. Finally I sat in the helm chair.

"You're careful," Jack said. "I like that."

"I've been almost dead. I learned to be careful," I replied.

"That tugboat thing?"

He had caught me by surprise. It had been almost ten years since inattention and a collision had left me treading water for more than three hours before another fishing boat had plucked me out of the ocean in deep hypothermia.

"I didn't know you knew about that. It was a while ago," I said.

"I make it a point to know about my crew."

"You're careful, too."

"I learned it the same way you did."

"Still, Jack, it's standard procedure."

"Yeah, but not everybody does it. I worry about the younger ones. It's easy to fall asleep when you're dog-assed tired. They've got a new thing I'm thinking of putting in. A red light goes on in front of you at random times. You've got five seconds to walk across the pilothouse and shut it off. A helmsman who falls asleep won't see it, and an alarm goes off. Then you fire the fucker."

"You've got a good crew, Jack. A good boat attracts a good crew. You don't need some red-light device, and you'll only piss them off."

Jack didn't say anything. He went down to get another cup of coffee. I never saw a man who could drink so much coffee. He would down two or three full pots and get so wired that he would yell and scream all the time, although it didn't seem to affect his judgment. One time he was going to turn the boat around from seventy miles out when the coffeemaker conked out, but I managed to rewire it and temporarily avert a crisis. Joe made sure we had a spare aboard after that trip.

Dave Preble

When Jack came back up he sat down and said, "I'm looking at a boat up in New Bedford." I didn't say anything, although I wasn't surprised. The JOHN AND JENNIFER was owned by a wealthy and politically well fixed attorney. The split was 50 percent for crew shares, minus crew expenses, and 50 percent for the owner, minus boat expenses. Jack got an additional 5 percent from the owner's share as captain and pretty much ran the boat the way he wanted to. But the boat still wasn't his, and with Jack's good track record and the easy credit of the times, it was inevitable that he would make the move. "I'll be taking some trips off to put it together, but Joe can run this boat, and there are a few good transit men around to fill out."

"You planning on taking the whole crew with you?"

"It's up to you guys," he said. "Joe will be offered this boat, or if he goes with me, Jim Moran wants it. Nobody's going to lose out. You going chartering with Linton again in the spring?"

"I don't know. I want my own boat, too. But a charterboat, not a dragger."

"Well, it may all work out then. I'll keep you posted." He finished his coffee and went below to sleep the rest of the way in.

Two hours later I went below, woke Jimmy, and turned the watch over to him. Then I bundled up, stepped out on deck, and walked up to the forepeak. A northwest breeze with a light chop slapped the bow as we moved into it. The sky was clear with bright stars, hard as diamonds, and the Milky Way stretched all the way across it; I stood there with the cold breeze in my face. The gibbous moon was just rising, and the winter sun would be only an hour or two behind it. It was December 1982, and not a one of us aboard knew that we were on one of the last really good trips that the F/V JOHN AND JENNIFER would ever make.

• • •

16

In 1976 the Magnuson Fisheries Conservation and Management Act (MFCMA) went into effect, extending the exclusive U.S. fishing zone to 200 miles from all U.S. coasts and setting up a framework for the management of all of our marine fisheries. Its first actual accomplishment was to curtail overfishing by the poorly regulated foreign fleets, and by 1978 the Cox Ledge rod-and-reel codfishing had once again gotten very good.

It didn't last. Under the guise of "helping" U.S. commercial fishermen expand into a perceived void left by the elimination of foreign competition, sweetheart legislation was passed to make it easy to build new technologically advanced vessels with government (read taxpayer) loan guarantees. What ensued was a feeding frenzy of speculation by starry-eyed fishermen and cynical bankers. Venture capitalists, lawyers, and businessmen with no knowledge of fishing but too much cash on their hands bankrolled boats in no-lose deals. Practically overnight the U.S. commercial fleet exploded with brand-new steel-hulled draggers, each with more electronic capabilities than the average World War II destroyer and more main engine power than the old-timers could even dream of. Even inshore lobster boats could get money to add on rollers and stacks of the new monofilament gillnets. At the same time, the management framework set up by the MFCMA was taken over by this hit-and-run crowd, while those who were supposed to blow the whistle sat back and rode the wave.

The result was a disaster. After a few years of some folks making lots of money killing lots of fish, the goose was exhausted and the golden eggs were gone. The cynical believe, with some reason, that the whole thing was planned from the very beginning by certain key politicians, in league with their banker friends, as nothing more than a cold-blooded raid on the federal treasury—and so what if some people got hurt. Whatever the actual chain of events and whoever was actually behind them, we are now left with an overcapitalized fleet (that's a banker's term—it means there are more than twice as many boats as the fisheries can support) and a devastated resource base (that's a bureaucrat's term—it means the fish are mostly dead), and the taxpayers are holding the bag. Most of the beautiful boats are now either in bankruptcy or close to it (for a while they were regularly being auctioned off to some poor dreamer who thought he could catch the million dollars per year worth of fish needed to support one of them). The bankers had their bets covered, so I guess they're still doing all right with the game.

The fish, though, aren't doing so well. Groundfish stocks have declined by more than 75 percent overall, with haddock in the worst shape at a decline of 95 percent. The fecund cod will probably recover their numbers if protected and allowed to, but the haddock may not. The trouble is that the balance between species has also been disrupted. The saleable demersals have been so hammered that the small bottom-dwelling shark known as the spiny dogfish and its cousin, the skate, have taken up the slack and exploded in numbers, going from 25 percent of the demersal biomass to around 80 percent in just over two decades.

The fishermen aren't doing so well either. I suppose they should have known better, but it's hard to see how they could have—the view from the deck of a boat is pretty restricted. After the foreign fleets left it was reasonable to see opportunity for expansion, and if the government wanted to guarantee a half-million dollar loan, go for it. Men who are normally independent by nature grabbed the bait, put up their homes for collateral, and went shopping. A few very lucky ones learned the rules of the real game being played by bankers and bureaucrats and did all right. Most did not. Many wound up losing their boats, their homes, and in too many cases their families and even their lives.

Everyone romanticizes the past to some extent. Americans maintain vestigial links to a perceived romantic past of rugged and colorful individuals through their attitudes toward cowboys, farmers, truck drivers, and commercial fishermen. The strength of these links has resulted in public policy that favors all four groups, which in turn has changed them into what they are today—workers in government-subsidized industries that are a long, long way from their romantic roots.

Commercial fishing still attracts the romantic dreamers and the social misfits. I suppose that going to sea in a small boat will always seem an adventure, no matter how few of the old skills survive the age of electronics or how little of the old rugged individualism survives the age of instant communications and Byzantine political resource management.

• • •

The sky was reddening in the east when I left the forepeak and went back into the deckhouse. "You were up there long enough," Jimmy yelled down from the pilothouse. "Don't you already get enough time on deck?"

I climbed the three steps into the pilothouse. "It's a beautiful morning, Jimmy."

"Yeah, but too fuckin' cold to stand up there in the wind. I can't wait to get *my* face between a couple of warm hooters."

"Yeah, but *your* trouble is you ain't *careful.* How many kids are you payin' for now?"

Jimmy frowned, "Just one. At least I don't marry 'em. How many times you been married, a half-dozen?"

"Three, and all happy marriages."

"Can't have been all that happy. Sounds fuckin' expensive to me."

"Ah, Jimmy, you just don't understand commitment. You're past help, and I gotta get some sleep." I started down the steps.

"Commitment, my ass," he yelled after me. "Tell that to your ex-wives!"

I slept through the day. When I awoke, the rest of the crew was up and the sun was almost down. We were only about an hour out, so I made up steak sandwiches, a panful of fried

---

potatoes, peppers, and onions, and a pot of fresh coffee. I was just finishing in the galley as we came through the outer breakwater into Point Judith. It was full dark, and Orion was bright in the eastern sky as we raised the outriggers before entering the inner harbor. We tied up at the dock under the bright lights and the hum of the conveyor belts and the shouts and blaring radios of the dock workers unloading—"taking out" they call it—other fishing boats. Once secured, we unrolled the net from the drum and started cleaning and mending it under Joe's supervision while Jack went up to the fishplant office to arrange for us to take out our fish.

It was more than an hour before he returned and with bad news. In the winter you can figure about thirty-six hours of calm between storms, and we had been hoping for a quick turnaround time for another good trip before the weather broke down. But there were three boats ahead of us, which, counting the one that had already started, meant at least a twelve-hour wait, even with two full take-out crews working. There was nothing we could do about this bottleneck, so we decided to finish up the deck work and go home for a few hours of R & R.

The next morning I got to the boat a little before six. I was the first to arrive, so I unlocked the deckhouse and started coffee and bacon. I was cooking onions and home fries when Jack, Joe, and the other Dave showed up. It was nine o'clock and we were just getting ready to move the boat into position at the end of the take-out dock when Jimmy showed up. He looked like hell, his eyes bloodshot and swollen and a large bruise on the side of his face. Jack laughed and said, "Well, I suppose every boat's gotta have at least one total fucking asshole, and on the JOHN AND JENNIFER it looks like you're it."

Jimmy ran his hand up through his hair, fingers spread out, as if the top of his skull was about to fly off and he was trying to hold it down. "I ran into Tommy, and we got into a fight outside the Dutch Inn," he said.

20

"What do the other guys look like?" I asked.

"No other guys. Tommy and I were fighting."

"Over what?" Jack asked. "I thought you two were friends?"

"Some slut, more 'n likely," Joe said.

"No. I don't remember," Jimmy said. "We had a few beers and got thrown out, and I don't know why we started swinging."

"A few beers?" Jack asked.

"We chased 'em with Wild Turkey."

Jack shook his head and pursed his lips, suddenly angry, and said, "Well, you can cool off your Wild Turkey in the hold today with the lumpers. And don't you puke on the fish! Let's move this boat over and get them out of it!"

The good lumpers had already worked around the clock, so we wound up paying four dollars per thousand pounds for a couple of kids who together couldn't even move eight thousand per hour. They were probably high-school dropouts who thought they were going to make big money. Jack kept screaming at them for poking holes in the fish with their pitchforks. It was four hours past sundown before we were done so we didn't give them any tip at all. As they left, one of them asked if I thought he could get a job on one of the boats. I just laughed.

We cleaned up on deck, hosed out the hold, and took on twelve thousand pounds of shaved ice. It was almost midnight before we cleared the outer breakwater, lowered the outriggers, and set a course to the edge of the continental shelf, ninety nautical miles out to sea. The marine weather forecast gave us about twenty-four hours before the next northeaster. It was going to be tight. If the weather forecaster was right and we found the butterfish right where they had been and we didn't make any mistakes, we wouldn't catch the brunt of the storm until we were well on our way back home. I made a pot of coffee and took a mug up to the pilothouse to begin my watch. The rest of the crew was all there except for Dave Barker, who was out on deck greasing the winches.

"We've been lucky with the weather," Joe said. "Maybe we can sneak this one in. At least if the butters haven't moved."

"Fuckin' lumpers hung us up," Jack said. "Fuckin' landsmen just don't get it."

"They want to be fishermen," I said. "One of them told me."

"Fishermen, my ass. Those two were dogshit. Too fuckin' dumb to be of any use on a boat." Jack wasn't very tolerant of inefficiency.

The weather held and the ride out was smooth, although after I got off watch I didn't sleep very well. At eight knots it was almost noon before we got to the grounds, and there were boats everywhere. "Looks like the word got out on these fish," Jack said. He zigzagged around for about twenty minutes, watching the blue screen of the fishfinder while the rest of us suited up; then he turned west along the ninety-fathom contour and slowed to idle speed. He opened the after pilothouse window and shouted, "Put the doors over. Run out the net. Two hundred seventy fathoms of wire." Dave One and I pushed the enormous iron doors out over the gunwales as Joe and Jimmy lifted them with the deck winches. Then Dave One ran the hydraulic controls on the starboard side of the net drum while I straightened the floats on the other side as the net rolled off and floated along behind the boat. We hooked the net to the doors, disconnected it from the drum, and stood back as Jack brought the main engine up to towing speed while Joe and Jimmy opened the winches and dropped the whole works to the bottom, carefully matching their speeds until the necessary scope of towing wire was out. Then they locked the winches, and we were fishing.

Jack set the autopilot and turned back again to the after pilothouse window, a dour expression on his face. "Twelve-minute tow," he shouted. "Let's see what's here. Set up the checkers for holds five and six."

Jimmy went below to lay a bed of ice in five and six while the rest of us dragged out the heavy cedar planks and got the deck ready. Then it was time to haul back the net. This process is basically just the reverse of shooting it out. Jack brought the boat down to idle speed while Joe and Jimmy ran the winches to retrieve the wire, the whole boat shuddering under the strain. When the doors came up Dave One and I switched the hooks from the doors to the net drum and then ran the net up onto the drum until we got to the bag end, which is where the fish wind up. Except that this time there wasn't very much in it.

Jack had put the boat on autopilot and was standing there when the bag came aboard. I snapped the puckering string and dropped the contents, maybe four hundred pounds of mixed species, onto the deck.

"Shit," Jack said. "All shit. Maybe a hundredweight saleable." He started back to the pilothouse.

"Shoot it again?" Joe asked.

"No, lemme look around a while," he answered.

We rode around for a half-hour while Jack scanned the bottom, sipping coffee, his eyes fixed on the glowing screen of the fishfinder. Finally he gave the order, and we set the net for a one-hour tow. By the time we went out on deck to haul back, the wind had gone northeast at about fifteen knots and the sky was gray and thickening. But we had twelve hundred pounds of mostly butterfish—not enough to get rich, but enough to work on and to make a trip out of. That is, if it held up and we had enough time.

Two tows later it was getting dark and the wind had passed twenty knots. The lights of the other boats looked like city streets at night. By eight o'clock the lights had thinned out as boats began the run to shelter, and the lights that still remained flickered as their boats rolled in the rising sea.

An hour later only two other boats were visible, and the wind was whistling in the rigging as we hauled back. The net held only six hundred pounds, barely half of which was butterfish. The fleet, which had swooped in, had decimated the schools, scattering what they had not taken. Jack gave the order to pull the doors aboard and to secure the net and all hatches. The wind had increased to more than thirty knots, and the bow was pitching as we turned north-northeast into the storm. And we hadn't even come close to covering our expenses.

The next three days passed in a numb haze of darkness, gray light, and darkness again. The first night we steamed to the "yellow hills," an area south of Martha's Vineyard. Nobody got much sleep, and by the time we arrived the wind was blowing a sustained forty knots with higher gusts and the sea was all white foam and crashing waves. But the island gave us enough protection so that we could work. The work, though, was what draggermen hate the worst and call "swilling." We made two-hour tows for whatever mixture the net captured and then spent most of the time between haulbacks on our hands and knees with a fishpick sorting it out, putting the saleable fish in baskets to later dump into whichever hold was designated for that species and flipping the unwanted fish over the side. Our best tow was twenty thousand pounds, but less than two thousand was saleable. The rest went back dead and covered the ocean in a line four miles long. Sometimes we would finish in time to grab something quick to eat before the next haulback. Many times we wouldn't, so the full net would be dumped into the fish already there and the rolling deck would be a foot deep in fish. For three days it went on, twenty-four hours a day. We ran four-handed so every fifth tow we each got off, but the noise and movement made it impossible to really sleep. Nobody spoke much, and there were no breaks in the routine except twice when we ripped the net and had to stop to repair it, hands stiff and ice in our beards.

By the third day the storm passed and the wind backed to the northwest, but it was colder and still blowing at twenty-five knots. That afternoon we were halfway through a tow when Jack suddenly yelled, "Haul back! Haul back!" as he brought the speed down to idle. We jumped to our stations and had started the winches turning when the boat was pulled to a near stop. "Shit!" Jack screamed. "Fuckin' dogfish! Saw 'em on the screen but it was too fuckin' late!" The winches strained, and the net finally came up—filled all the way to the wing ends with more than eighty thousand pounds of spiny dogfish sharks, their dorsal spines wrapped in the mesh. Jack brought the engine up to eleven hundred rpm, and the whole thing planed out behind us. He set the autopilot and came out on deck. "We got ourselves a real problem here," he said, his mouth pulled tight over his teeth.

"Think we can split and hoist 'em?" Joe asked. Split and hoist is a process for emptying a very full net in sections.

"I don't think so. Spines will hang up. But let's try it."

Jack went up to man the Pullmaster electric winch, and we brought the first section aboard but the spines of the packed dogs were all locked together under the pressure, and we couldn't empty them out. Finally we dropped the whole mess back into the ocean and Jack came back down on deck.

"We're going to have to cut the net," he said, "and someone's going to have to walk back on it to do it. We'll draw straws."

"Fuck straws," Joe said. "I'll do it. One of you sharpen up a knife and lash it good to a broomhandle." Joe went below and put on a lifejacket, and we tied a hundred-foot length of half-inch line around his waist. Then we payed it out as he walked out on that net streaming behind the boat in the winter sea. When he got to the end of the net he jammed the knife into it and started running back to the boat, slicing mesh, the dogfish escaping and the net collapsing behind him. As he reached the chute he slipped and fell, and we dragged him up onto the deck.

We spent the next four hours, into the dark, repairing and cleaning the cut net. When we finished and rolled the last of it onto the net drum Jack looked around at our pale faces and red eyes and said, "What a sorry-assed bunch. This crew has had it. Let's go home."

When the settlement was made we had covered expenses and the share for each crewman was just under two hundred dollars for the trip. The next trip Jack took off to set up the deal for his own boat. A month later he left the JOHN AND JENNIFER and took the crew with him—except for me. I stayed a month with the new captain and crew and then took two weeks in South Florida baking the winter cold out of my bones. By then the charter season had started so I went back to work on a charterboat. A year later I had my own charterboat. Joe Mendes stayed with Jack for a short time and then was hired to run a boat for another rich lawyer. Three years later his left leg was torn off at the knee in a winch accident. Dave Barker bought a small inshore dragger so he could day fish and spend nights at home. He worked hard and did well for a while, but declining fish stocks and increasing regulations started to hurt him, and the last I heard he was looking for a shore job. Jimmy Lang finally did get married. He bought a house and had three more kids, but got overextended and started doing amphetamines so he could make every trip. He and his wife separated, and then one night he came in from a trip and went down to a lonely stretch of rocky shore with a bottle of whiskey and a .38 Special. He drank half the bottle and then put the gun in his mouth and pulled the trigger.

The JOHN AND JENNIFER also met a bad end. In the last month I was on her with the new crew we worked hard and did all right. One trip we towed through a slough between two of the Nantucket Shoals and got sixteen thousand pounds of cod. We made a second tow over the same ground while we ripped and gutted all those fish and netted another eighteen hundred pounds, but a third tow netted less than two hundred pounds, so I guess we got them all. Another time we worked the Lent-driven market for whiting for two good trips before the price crashed. But for the most part we ended the winter swilling, and there was never a really good year after that. Soon the new captain put up his home and bought his own boat, and then the JOHN AND JENNIFER went through a couple of more captains and crews. Along the line she became known as a haven for druggies, and it was said that her maintenance was slipping, things that would not have been tolerated in her better days. She was in the news when a young crewman died in his berth from a heroin overdose after four days at sea, and then a month later she was coming in from a winter trip when something apparently happened that caused what is known in the business as a CLS, or catastrophic loss of stability. The F/V JOHN AND JENNIFER rolled over and sank with all hands. No messages were sent, and no one knows where she now lies.

CHAPTER 2

Yankees; Boat Gremlins; Gender Equity;
First Trip; Weather

The people along the sand
All turn and look one way.
They turn their back on the land
They look at the sea all day.
—Robert Frost, *The Poems of Robert Frost,* 1946

Robert Frost's poems have appealed to people across many lands and cultures because they explore universal themes. But the regional flavor of collections such as Frost's *North of Boston* illustrates how groups of people can also possess unique characteristics and shared values, formed and bound by geography and environment, and that Frost understands the people "north of Boston" to form such a group.

People from other regions of the country have always considered New Englanders to be of a type, characterized by the old clichés: cold, distant, frugal, reticent, dry-humored. Many years ago I took a job as a ranger in Yellowstone National Park. At the end of the first season my supervisor, who was from the West Coast, wrote in my work evaluation that I had done "a commendable job" but added that my only fault was "an apparent lack of warmth and friendliness in dealing with the public." He went on to say that I was "polite but distant," but he allowed that this was "characteristic of the region he comes from."

If it is true that I lack "warmth and friendliness," the reason has little to do with the region I come from. What Robert Frost knew so well, but my western supervisor was unaware of, is that New England consists of two regions, and the dividing line between them is "north of Boston." The classic New England Yankee of the clichés is an inland creature, formed by big woods and small farms, hills and mountains, and long, cold, snowy winters. He is politically conservative, socially progressive in a strictly local sense, and suspicious of change, particularly that which arises from the outer world.

The other New England, "south of Boston," is formed by the ocean and its effects on the land, the climate, and the people. Geographically, it includes all of Connecticut, Rhode Island, and Massachusetts south of a line from the Berkshires to Boston. But it also extends northward along the coast and inland to a line running roughly through Leominster, Massachusetts, and Rochester, New Hampshire. This band of southern New England culture narrows in Maine, where it includes Portland and ends at Penobscot Bay. Beyond the Penobscot, the coastal people have retained the north country Yankeeness, but with more than a little of coastal Canada thrown in.

The people of the southern New England coastal band are different from those "north of Boston" in some fundamental ways. They are urban, gregarious, and garrulous. Where northern Yankees feel a bond to the land from which they arose, southern New Englanders "turn their back on the land" and "look at the sea all day." Ocean commerce builds their cities, fuels their industries, and brings the immigrants that make their populations polyglot and multiethnic, their society cosmopolitan but also restless. Even those who claim no affinity with the sea are economically and culturally dominated by it.

I suppose that one can make too much of the cultural differences between northern and southern New Englanders since, as those of us who have passed our fiftieth birthday have seen, the movement of history over the past half-century has moderated differences among groups of people everywhere. The world of Robert Frost's Yankees "north of Boston" is certainly shrinking, driven in from its edges by urbanization and changed from within by the homogenizing effect of television. But even so, southern New Englanders still generally consider their northern brethren to be quaint country bumpkins, and northern New Englanders are still regularly heard referring to their southern brethren, with unmistakable derision, as "flatlanders."

The effect of the ocean on southern New England is not just cultural, but also climatic, and the two are intertwined. Winter in the inland north is long and cold, with dry air and much snow, and the people who live there love it. I once saw a sign on a Vermont storefront that stated, with obvious pride:

WELCOME TO VERMONT

NINE MONTHS OF WINTER

AND

THREE MONTHS OF LOUSY SKIING

Such a sentiment would never be expressed in the coastal south, where it seems everyone expresses a deep hatred of winter and complains incessantly throughout the season. The northern Yankee saves for a new snowmobile, while the southern New Englander saves for a midwinter trip to Florida, or if he can't afford it, at least talks about it a lot. A New Hampshire contractor I used to know once hired some men from Connecticut and Rhode Island to work through the winter. By the end of January he wanted to fire the lot. "All these goddamn flatlanders do is bitch about the weather," he told me. "Hell, if they don't like the winter they shouldn't be in New England." I couldn't make him understand that "bitching about the weather" is a cultural staple of southern New England and that he shouldn't take it quite so seriously.

There is good reason for the southern New England attitude. Winter is a dreary time along the coast. It is long enough, cold enough, and damp enough to bring people to near-depression. The damp dreariness is caused by the effects of the ocean. The huge mass of heat-absorbing water moderates coastal temperatures and, while it cools summer's heat, it also prevents the dry cold of a true northern winter. While the cold isn't as deep, the dampness makes its effects severe. I once saw forty below in northern Maine, but never in my life felt as frigid as one morning on Cape Ann when the temperature was almost fifty degrees higher but the northeast wind from the North Atlantic drove the damp cold right through my bones.

The trouble is, coastal winters aren't reliable. You may get just enough snow to drag the cross-country skis out of the closet and just enough pond ice for a few days of skating—just enough to pique your interest and stir your blood—and then three days of cold drizzle set in and ruin it. And if you work Monday through Friday, the few good winter weather days seem always to be early in the workweek. Then, after you wait all week to get out, along comes the icy rain for the weekend. But there I go, bitching like a flatlander.

• • •

Winters along the coast don't really begin until after the holidays. The charterboats fish for striped bass at least until Thanksgiving, and December is a good month for cod and tautog. Since the ocean water temperature doesn't really tumble until around Christmas, the bitter weather usually holds off until the end of the month or later. So making it into the new year is easy. Then the drearies set in and last until sometime after St. Patrick's Day.

As a charterboat captain, St. Patrick's Day marks the end of my dreary time. There may be more snow and cold drizzle, but the sun has become stronger, the days definitely longer, daytime temperatures noticeably higher. The inside work of winter is done.

Reels are serviced, new rods are built and old ones repaired, new gear is made. Now the boat occupies center stage. From St. Patrick's Day until the first charter, a month later, is the most frenetic time of the year. The bottom is sanded and painted, nicks and dings in the hull repaired and then the whole hull waxed and buffed, the engine wire-brushed and touched up, pump impellers replaced, hydraulic system serviced, shaft alignment adjusted, zincs installed, topsides and deck sanded and painted, wiring inspected and repaired, electronics reinstalled and tested, and dozens of other minor repairs made.

There are certain immutable natural laws that apply whenever work is done on a boat. Here are a few:

1. Every job on a boat takes at least five times longer than you think it will and three times longer than it should.

2. Parts for a boat are marked up at least twice as much as parts for any other mechanical device on the theory that anyone who owns a boat must be wealthy and expects to pay a lot.

3. The second law also applies to commercial boats because anyone who works on a boat must have a very high income that he is largely hiding from the tax man. This is true even if he has filed bankruptcy because that is also probably some sort of tax dodge.

4. During each day of work on a boat you need at least one tool that you forgot to bring. This costs you a minimum of two hours either retrieving yours or finding one to borrow.

5. During every job you drop at least one tool, bolt, nut, or other object.

6. Every tool, bolt, nut, or other object you drop tends to seek the deepest and least accessible point in the bilge.

7. Nothing that needs to be worked on is ever easy to get to. Boats are designed with this principle in mind.

8. Any day that you have to paint in order to stay on schedule it rains. Always.

9. You are never 100 percent ready for the first trip of the year. Even if you think you are.

10. Boat gremlins are real. They were once described to me by a towboat captain as "little mythic creatures who get on your boat in the winter and fuck things up."

• • •

Several years ago a local marina hired a woman about thirty-five years old to work the counter in the parts department. She was friendly and smiled at everyone and asked many questions in a sincere effort to learn. This commendable characteristic earned her nothing but abuse, and she became something of a target. One day a charterboat captain came in and asked her for four stainless wingnuts. She smiled in her usual way and asked him what they looked like and where she might find them. He affected a smart-assed smirk and said, "They look like little bugs with their wings out, and you find them bouncing around up near the ceiling. Sometimes they get caught in spider webs." The dock rats and fishermen who heard this remark thought it was very funny, and from that point on her nickname became Wingnut.

A few days later I went in and told her I needed some "sacrificial anodes." She gave me the smile and said, "What do they look like?"

"Zincs," I answered.

"Over in the last aisle," she said. I went over and picked out two shaft zincs and brought them to the counter. "What did you call them?" she asked.

"Sacrificial anodes."

"Oh. Why are they called that?"

"Because we put them on our boats as a sacrifice to the boat gremlins. They eat these things, and if we keep them fed they don't come on our boats and fuck things up." I could hear the snickers around me.

Her smile never faded. Not one bit. "You really *are* an asshole, aren't you?" she said.

"Yeah, I guess I am," I answered in my best bantering tone.

"I had heard that about you, but I didn't believe it until now." She put her arm around the other counter worker. "From now on, I'll just direct my questions to Ron. He doesn't use his knowledge to try to embarrass me. Also, he's younger and better looking than most of you other jerks." Ron was smirking, and her sweet smile had never missed a beat, though her voice had taken on a bit of an edge.

When I left with my "sacrificial anodes" I was thinking that when I was young a woman would never have called a man an asshole to his face, even when it was entirely appropriate. But then a man would never have used the word "fuck" in front of a woman. I guess that's gender equity. The last I heard, Wingnut was still working around fishermen and still holding her own.

• • •

During the winter I lose track of the other charterboat captains. Some have shore jobs, some take boats south, some hit the fishing show circuit. But, whatever else they do, like all fishermen their identity derives more from their boats than from any other aspect of their lives. There are men with whom I have a speaking acquaintance without ever really knowing their names. But if someone says, "You know so-and-so, he has the Laura Jane," then I know exactly whom he means.

Most charter captains are vain and jealous misfits who use high-tech electronic gadgets yet are pretty much out of place in the post-millennial world. My wife calls us "a bunch of overgrown schoolboys," and most of us certainly show a strong strain of immaturity in our rivalries and our inability to accept bosses, regulations, or any form of outside authority. When the boat work starts in the spring I regain contact with this world, and its petty rivalries, nasty gossip, and hard-edged banter begin anew.

The first of the boat work is generally accompanied by visitations, exchanges of news and gossip, and a lot of coffee breaks. Later, as launch day approaches with a realization that there is still a hell of a lot to do, it all gets very serious. Finally the last sacrificial anode is screwed into place, and the Travelift is ready to splash the boat. Nervous, I ride the boat down in the slings to the old familiar magic as the hull touches water and I feel the deck move as decks are supposed to move. Boats belong in the water.

The first trip of the year is different from any other. There is an uncertain, new feeling, no matter how many years you have on the water. Part of this uncertainty is due to the newness of so much of your operation. The boat is clean and painted, there is some new gear, and what isn't new is all clean and freshly serviced. Another part results from being ashore for as long as four months. You are uneasy because you don't really know everything the boat gremlins might have done.

There is also the feeling of lifting to your shoulders a familiar load that had been set down. A charterboat captain is, quite simply, responsible for the safety of everyone on his vessel. This responsibility not only includes maintaining and operating a safe vessel, but also extends to controlling dangerous behavior in his passengers. Maritime law recognizes that passengers (who are not what is called "prudential seamen") are in an unfamiliar and potentially dangerous environment and therefore places responsibility for their safety on the shoulders of a licensed captain. This is why, for instance, most captains limit the amount or type of liquor on board and carefully, if not obviously, monitor passengers' alcohol intake. A hard-drinking charter group is never taken to the best fishing and may find themselves back at the dock early.

The safety record of charterboats is excellent—the best of any user group afloat. This record is reflected in the low insurance rates the industry enjoys at a time when other types of commercial vessels are plagued by astronomical rates. Charterboat captains are licensed by the U.S. Coast Guard after passing a tough test and certifying their experience. It is unusual to see a charterboat captain commit an unsafe or negligent act of poor seamanship. Commercial trawlers, on the other hand, have a terrible safety record that is steadily getting worse and is resulting in an insurance crisis in their industry. There are many reasons to account for their problems, but it is a fact that no license is required of anyone to captain a trawler of under 300 tons (which includes most of the East Coast dragger fleet), and it is common to observe grossly unsafe practices aboard them. Although the better trawler captains are fine seamen, there are too many who are not, and at least one national commercial fishing publication has lamented the fact that too many of today's commercial fishing boats are being captained by men who are "superb technicians in the skills of fishing but poor seamen."

I point this out not to denigrate trawler captains (my father was one, and I have worked on trawlers) or to lionize charterboat captains (not all are honest or even competent fishermen) but to call attention to the value of a tough licensing policy for people who so clearly hold the lives of others in their hands. As a general rule I am quite suspicious of governmental regulation, but for the safety of those who venture onto the ocean, the value of licensing vessel captains is clearly established and beyond dispute.

• • •

People from northern and southern New England may differ in their attitudes toward the weather, but weather is the one thing that dominates every boat captain's life. When I get up in the morning, even before I turn on the coffee, I check the barometer, the thermometer, the wind direction and speed, and I turn on the VHF weather channel. This ritual is so ingrained that I even continue it when the boat is laid up for the winter. Before I go to bed at night I check the daily weather map to monitor in my mind the march of weather systems across the country.

The decision not to sail or to terminate a trip due to weather is an important one for a charterboat captain and not solely because of safety. If he cancels a day that later proves fishable, he loses both credibility and money. If he "goes out in anything," he may save a day's pay, but he loses dissatisfied customers to his competition. After all, people charter a boat to have fun, not to get beaten up by rough seas.

Most captains wait to make weather cancellations until the morning of the trip, with the customers on the dock. This delay may seem inconsiderate, but there are two reasons for it. First, predictions of exact sea conditions are difficult to make very far in advance. Second, parties are different in their tolerance of rough weather. I am quicker to cancel a trip if I can see that a group is tender than if they are hardy. I may even go out a few miles on a rough day before I make a judgment. So although making the decision sooner may save a charter group some travel time, I am reluctant to cancel ahead of time unless it is a dead certainty that the weather will be dangerously rough.

The most important weather factor is the wind, because the wind generates waves, and big enough waves can destroy a boat and kill its crew and passengers. Waves may be driven by wind (swell and surf) or the gravitational attraction between the earth, sun and moon (tides). Waves are complex, as is the weather, and can be long or short, high or low, steep or gentle. For example, a storm way offshore in deep water frequently develops very high waves that are also very long (the length of a wave, or wavelength, is the distance from crest to crest between succeeding waves), so they have a gentle slope. These waves are called swells when they move into shallower water far from the storm that caused them, and a boat easily rides up and over them, even if they are so high that the vessel disappears completely from view in the trough between. On the other hand, wind from shallower to deeper water develops lower waves, but they may be more dangerous since they are short and steep, a condition referred to as choppy. There are other wave patterns, some of which are quite complex and may overlap from different directions, to produce what is called a "confused" or "cranky" sea. A cranky sea is fatiguing, since your body cannot adapt to the unpredictable, irregular movement it imparts to a boat.

Furthermore, overlapping wave trains can be either in or out of phase with one another, a state that can change from moment to moment depending upon the length and direction of the waves in each train. When they are out of phase the effects of their energies upon one another are subtractive, and the sea is momentarily flattened. But when they are in phase, the effects are additive, producing a series of waves, usually two or three, of above average height. Once in a great while the addition of effects is nearly perfect, producing a "freak wave," which is defined by the U.S. National Weather Service as "a wave of great height and steepness, much higher than other waves in the prevailing sea or swell system." The old-timers used to refer to a wave of this type as "a queer one" and made little of it.

The ultimate height to which waves grow is a function of the velocity of the wind, the length of time that it blows, and the fetch, or span of open water that it can act upon. The National Weather Service describes prevailing sea states with the statistical term "significant wave height" (SWH), which is defined as the average vertical distance from the trough to the crest of the highest third of the expected waves. Starting from a flat calm sea on the open ocean, a fifty-knot wind generates an SWH of nineteen feet in about five hours. But if the same wind blows steadily for twenty hours, the SWH will reach forty feet! And the probability is that one wave in every thousand will be a "queer one" of twice the SWH, or about eighty feet. To place that statistic in perspective, if the period between waves is about ten seconds, a freak wave of twice the SWH can be expected on an average of once every three hours.

Ferocious sea conditions came to the forefront of public consciousness with the release of the movie version of Sebastian Junger's book, *The Perfect Storm,* about the loss of the F/V ANDREA

GAIL with her entire crew on the Atlantic Ocean in October 1991. Most everyone agreed that the movie's special effects were spectacular, but could waves actually get that big? They can. The Halloween northeaster, as the storm was then known to meteorologists, lasted for three days and produced peak continuous winds of around seventy knots (eighty miles per hour) in the area of the last known position of the ANDREA GAIL. Seventy knots is a lot of wind, but it certainly breaks no records. However, it blew at that velocity for more than twenty-four hours, or twice as long as would be expected at any single location in a typical northeaster. The SWH in the area where the ANDREA GAIL was lost would have been greater than sixty feet for a full day, with at least a few waves of twice that height. The "perfect storm" never reached landfall, but the National Weather Service has called it the "benchmark storm for the open waters of the northwest Atlantic in the second half of the twentieth century."

The term "rogue wave" is commonly used and much loved by the media, particularly that part of it given to sensationalism, but it has no real meaning to a seaman, although I have heard it used by some who had lost boats through either negligence or simple human error. The very term "rogue" implies something outside of the normal laws of physics and even a bit supernatural. I know that this remark will anger some who read it, but in nearly five decades on the ocean, although I have seen many large and scary freak waves—the "queer ones" that the prudent seaman expects occasionally—I have never seen any wave that I would call a rogue, nor have I ever heard a reliable report from anyone else who has ever seen such a thing.

The wave-producing winds travel out of regions of high pressure and into regions of low pressure. These regions are part of weather systems that develop from a complicated combination of heating differences in different parts of the atmosphere; the earth's rotation; the characteristics of mountains, seas, and lakes; and even the activities of man. With study a boat captain learns the general patterns of the weather and the winds. With experience he learns how they apply to his area.

• • •

The U.S. National Weather Service takes a lot of unfair criticism from people who don't know what they are talking about. The truth is that, although it experienced some growing pains in the eighties, the service today scores high marks for organizing huge amounts of data and disseminating it widely in useful forecasts over large areas. It is important to remember that the earth's atmosphere is dynamic and complex and our understanding of it is very new and still incomplete.

Before World War II, weather forecasting was neither reliable nor particularly useful to fishermen and other marine users. As a result, every captain became his own forecaster (hence the myth of the old fisherman being a "weather expert"), and coastal fishing boats were constructed to withstand heavy pounding and to allow storm-driven seas to wash right over them. But this self-reliance was accompanied by a tolerance of loss the order of which we do not accept today. In an autumn gale in 1837 Cape Cod lost seventy-eight fishermen and their boats. In 1841 another gale claimed the lives of eighty-seven, and in September of 1846 eleven Marblehead boats went down with sixty-five men. One of the very worst storms recorded in the northeast was the Minot's Light Gale, or as it was sometimes called, the Yankee Gale, in October 1851. The total losses from that one will never be known, but after it was over the shores from New England to Prince Edward Island were strewn with washed up wreckage and the bodies of drowned fishermen.

These types of losses, along with late nineteenth-century growth in foreign trade, brought about the establishment of the U.S. Weather Bureau in 1890. But knowledge of the atmosphere was primitive, and major storms went unpredicted even up to the eve of World War II a half-century later. Anyone much over the age of sixty-five remembers the famous 1938 hurricane that roared into New England with no warning at all and devastated the coast, killing hundreds.

With the coming of World War II and the need to send millions of troops and hundreds of ships across thousands of miles of oceans, accurate weather prediction suddenly became vital to national survival. The military services bought new equipment, funded new research, trained new forecasters, and enormously expanded our knowledge of the workings of the atmosphere. When the war ended, demobilization provided a pool of trained people as the old U.S. Weather Bureau quickly grew to meet the needs imposed by new foreign commitments and new economic growth, particularly in the weather-sensitive areas of agriculture, commercial fishing, and overseas shipping.

In 1970 the bureau was reorganized, renamed the National Weather Service, and placed under the newly created National Oceanic and Atmospheric Administration (NOAA). Over the next few years forecasts were timely and generally reliable. Veteran forecasters had added experience to their earlier training—art joined science. I remember those days, working on a dragger, sitting out a wintertime storm in port, setting an alarm clock every three hours through the night to listen to the weather radio. Forecast updates used to be on at two, five, eight, and eleven, around the clock, and we relied upon them to give us the precise time when we could slip out into the waning storm, beating other boats to the fish and back to get the highest price for our catch.

This golden era didn't last, and in the eighties the weather service fell on hard times. Its budget suffered a series of cuts at the same time that outdated equipment began to break down and the most experienced postwar personnel began to retire. Also, there was a general belief in the executive branch that the National Weather Service should be privatized, or at the very least self-supporting. Traditional weather service functions were questioned and often assigned elsewhere; no one seemed to have a clear idea of who should do what. Forecast accuracy dropped along with the service's reputation. The weather service was even sued after an unpredicted ocean squall claimed an offshore lobster boat and most of its crew. The suit failed in court, but it was widely reported and discussed among fishermen. For almost a decade the National Weather Service's dockside ratings were very low, and the weather entries in my logbooks for those years chronicle the decline. One scientific journal rated U.S. weather reports and forecasts as "the worst in the western world."

Something had to be done. Weather forecasting means more than letting the population know if it can play golf this weekend—it is a vital component in daily decisions in a variety of industries involving an astronomical amount of money and the livelihoods of millions of people. So in 1987 the National Research Council (NRC) of the National Academy of Sciences appointed a committee of distinguished individuals from industry, university, and government to "investigate opportunities to improve marine forecasting."

The NRC published a report in 1989 that was both revealing in its findings and specific in its recommendations. The number one finding was that there had been a breakdown in NOAA's management. "Who's in charge?—All too frequently, the committee was unable to identify the person or agency clearly and singly responsible for operation of the observing and forecasting system and end user support." It recommended a management overhaul and a clear designation of policies. The committee found much that was good and suggested a number of technical recommendations, but emphasized that the implementation of new technologies would be "difficult or impossible" without improved management.

The enormous importance of accurate weather forecasting had created a mandate for change, and the report served as a blueprint. The NRC formed a separate advisory group called the National Weather Service Modernization Committee to help in directing the changes. From the beginning the committee has kept the process open by seeking input from all the user groups through regional citizens advisory boards (I am a member of the New England Marine Weather Advisory Board), thus making certain that adopted priorities reflect real needs. It seems to have struck a proper balance between what should be done by private companies and paid for by specific users and what should be done by government and paid for by the taxpayers.

My logbook weather entries since the beginning of the 1990s show the result—a steady improvement in forecast accuracy. Part of the reason for the improvement is the skillful application of new technologies, such as high-speed computers (the Advanced Weather Interactive Processing System, or AWIPS), Doppler radar (NEXRAD or WSR-88D), and geostationary (GOES) satellites. There have also been advances in understanding and modeling the dynamics of the atmosphere. But the biggest reason is improvement in the administration of the agency itself. Morale is up, and the service has been able to hire some of the most talented and well educated of the younger meteorologists and atmospheric physicists. It has been more than a decade since the NRC report, and the U.S. National Weather Service once again knows what it is doing and where it is going.

Of course, all is not perfect—there have been enormous improvements, but the weather service is, and always will be, subject to the same pressures as any other government agency. And there are still large gaps in our understanding of the atmosphere. It is still hard to predict how fast weather systems move, particularly during the spring and autumn when the atmosphere is rapidly changing. Another problem, which has so far proven intractable, is predicting the location and intensity of violent local squalls that can arise on the ocean due to intense heat gradients. The newspapers, replete with stories of destruction and death, refer to them as "freak squalls," but the correct name is "explosive cyclogenesis," or "bomb squalls," and little is known about the exact conditions in which they develop.

The worst bomb squall I ever experienced occurred in the summer of 1996. Surface wind increased from ten knots to measured gusts as high as eighty-two knots in less than seven minutes. I jogged my boat into it, clawing for sea room to keep from being driven onto the rocks of Block Island. Yet, when the associated front passed boats just eight miles away, the wind peaked at less than twenty-five knots. Four small boats were capsized, and I heard some pointed criticism of the weather service, but it had issued earlier warnings of a strong approaching front with unstable conditions, and it is hard for me to imagine that the forecasters could have done any better. I was in the middle of it, and the term "bomb" is an accurate one. The squall arose suddenly over a small area and subsided just as quickly.

Most of today's complaints are nothing more than the obligatory lamentations of flatlanders who will forever complain about the weather and, by association, the weather service. Experienced seamen may also play the game, but deep down they know better. National Weather Service forecasts are high-quality and very useful, and the knowledgeable captain uses them as a guide, knowing that responsibility for the safety of the vessel is his alone and the decision to sail or to return to port because of the weather is similarly his alone.

CHAPTER 3

Customers; Mal de Mer; Government,
Fish, and the Social Fabric; THE OUTLAW

A fisherman's hopes are of the future and his joys are of the
present.
—Zane Grey, *Tales of Swordfish and Tuna*, 1927

The first trip of the year for a Swamp Yankee charterboat is almost always a codfishing trip. Some time between late March and mid-April cod migrate from their wintering ground in deep water up onto Cox Ledge and the rock piles south of Block Island, and it is this movement that begins the charter season. (There are also some fish, locally called "groundkeepers," which either overwinter on the ledge or at least move over it during the cold months, and provide a winter fishery for the larger head boats.)

Cox Ledge is hilly, rising to a depth of only fifteen fathoms in spots (one fathom is six feet). Its rocks and coarse gravel provide homes for enormous numbers of invertebrates that attract several species of demersal fish, including not only the cod but also ocean pout, pollock, hake, whiting, spiny dogfish, and skate. Years ago there were also a few haddock (enough to constitute about one of every ten fish of my boat's catch), but the last haddock I caught on Cox Ledge was in early 1983. I don't know if their disappearance south of Cape Cod is a result of their devastation on Georges Bank or some change in their migration or in the ocean itself of which we are unaware. Migrating pelagics also often show up on Cox Ledge in the spring, starting with the mackerel and bluefish and followed by shark, tuna, and marlin. But the ledge is best known for its codfishing.

Just as the demersals are fundamentally different from the pelagics, the rod-and-reelers who charter boats in pursuit of particular species are fundamentally different. The typical groundfish charter is a blue-collar male from the middle or lower middle class who works for a paycheck and sees a direct relationship between effort and reward. He enjoys his fishing, but his success is measured by the poundage of fillets he takes home at the end of the day. He is politically conservative and xenophobic and views world events as straightforward interactions between personalities. He may have traveled afar in the armed forces, but today rarely goes farther than an occasional fishing trip within a day's drive from home. He may go fishing to "get away from the old lady" (or girl friend) but then spends a good part of the day talking about women or telling sexually explicit jokes. Groundfishermen are generally hardy and tolerant of wet, cold weather and a pitching deck while anchored in a sloppy sea. They are less tolerant of long boat rides and long waits for fish. And these characteristics hold true even when they decide to book a trip to try for offshore pelagics (big game) such as shark or tuna.

Charters for shark, tuna, and billfish tend to be upper-middle-class white-collar types, either professional or middle management. Their groups often include women (groundfishing groups almost never do), who are generally articulate and outspoken and are often skilled anglers. The members of these groups see the trip more as an adventure than a way to fill the freezer and will break off from fishing for an hour or more to photograph whales, dolphins, or a large basking shark. They are tolerant and range the political spectrum, are interested in foreign affairs, and see world events as complex interactions among historical imperatives. They enjoy travel and have usually sampled the fishing in more locations than most charter captains, although there is often surprisingly little depth to their experience. Many own expensive fishing equipment, and a few are skilled in its use, although far fewer than think they are. These groups don't mind long boat rides and don't panic if the fish are slow in coming. They are conservation minded and won't hesitate to release extra fish, particularly if they can be tagged first.

Of course, not all groups fit into neat categories. I also have a few aging hippies, a sort of laid-back group of hunter-gatherers who equate fishing, philosophically, with picking blueberries or repairing an old pickup truck. They enjoy their charter trips but see the whole experience as a sort of grand cycle of which they are a small part.

Occasionally I get charter groups that can be categorized by nationality or race. Given our nation's polyglot history with its ethnic and racial divisions, these trips can be uneasy and occasionally embarrassing. I had a group of Polish immigrants and first-generation Polish-Americans out codfishing during the time of the Solidarity movement and the Gdansk shipyard strikes for Polish independence, and every member of the group wore large white SOLIDARNOSC buttons. Their talk all day was of Lech Walesa, Soviet intransigence, and the future of what they hoped would be a free Poland. Early in the afternoon we anchored over a wreck, and the fish started biting. I had left the radio on, low enough not to be intrusive but loud enough so I could hear it on deck. Busy with gaffing and bleeding fish, I paid no attention to it until I noticed that the whole group had gone quiet. Suddenly, with horror, I realized that one of the other charter captains was on the radio, telling the most offensive Polish joke that I had ever heard then or have ever heard since. By their flushed faces and glaring eyes I knew that these people were deeply offended (as they should have been). I dropped the gaff, ran to the radio, and punched the off button. Walking back on deck, shaking my head, my lips tight, I didn't know what I could possibly say, so I said nothing. It was a beautiful day and the fishing was good, but the joy had gone out of it. Nowadays, I usually leave the radio off—remembering a bunch of good guys from whom I never heard again.

I also have groups of African-Americans who fish with me. I am not talking here about individual blacks who come as members of mixed groups but of groups that are made up of only black members. This is tough to write about because, although I can freely discuss yuppie groups, or redneck groups, or even Polish groups, every time I mention a black group in public, someone, always a white person, takes offense in a way that strikes me as both pious and guilt-laden. But the fact is that black groups who charter my boat are as different from white groups as blue-collar groups are from the yuppies. They are open and relaxed and seem able to easily shed their worldly cares when they step aboard. While a typical white group may be a smile and a chuckle, a typical black group is a belly laugh. Their ballbusting of one another is brutal, although good-natured and accompanied by much laughter. Losing a fish, catching fewer than anyone else, and especially getting seasick—all are targets for detailed and hilarious comment by the others.

Excluded from this camaraderie, however, is the white captain. I don't believe it is racism, either black or white. The open friendliness of black charters toward me is both obvious and genuine, and I was brought up in a Yankee family, descended from abolitionist Unitarians who believed that the soul had no color and that all men should be judged, in Dr. Martin Luther King's words, "by the content of their character." Yet, all that having been said, none of us can escape history. In every black group there are always one or two whose eyes reveal to me something, but what? A deep, underlying hatred? Perhaps, but I am not sure; it may be simply the pain of personal experience and racial history, but it is fatuous to deny its existence. Despite mutual respect and regard, there is a barrier between the black charter group and the white captain.

Sometimes we can reach through the barrier. A group of black men who had fished with me for a decade arrived at the boat one morning a couple of years ago for their annual codfish trip. The leader of the group waited until everyone was aboard and within earshot and then said to me, "Cap'n Dave"—he always called me that—"Cap'n Dave, what's white and twelve inches long?"

I thought a moment, then said, "I don't know, Jim, what is?"

Shaking his head, he looked at me and said, "Not a thing, man, not a thing in the world!"

Everyone on the boat erupted in laughter, and I felt that, however temporarily, a wall had been breached.

• • •

Unfortunately, on a boat the reality of *mal de mer* cannot be denied, although for obvious public relations reasons, many charter captains downplay it as much as possible. Some actually try to pretend that it doesn't exist: "Oh, don't worry. It almost never happens on my boat." Others offer helpful advice: "If you feel discomfort, you should [insert some home remedy]." Others belittle it, and still others ignore the subject completely. One captain I know has a sign above the toilet that reads "No puking in head." Still another, whose business includes a lot of drifting for cod, has a sign just aft of the deckhouse on the port side that reads "Puke station." By habitually positioning the boat to drift with the port side downwind, he is able to keep vomit out of the boat.

I tend to be rather sanguine about seasickness, avoiding discussing it on the theory that one should let sleeping dogs lie. When someone is overcome, I try to be optimistic about the prognosis, although in reality I rarely see anyone recover until his or her feet are on firm ground. My problem is a lack of empathy—I have never been seasick.

I was close once, about twenty years ago, although it was my own fault. I was working as mate on the charterboat MAKO II out of Snug Harbor, Rhode Island, for Captain Bob Linton. I had been invited to a wedding that I knew was going to be a very gala affair and wanted the next day off to recover. My troubles began when I couldn't find anyone to cover for me, so I had to be on the boat at five-thirty in the morning. On the night of the wedding, a northeast storm blew in with high winds and sheets of rain, and I went to the wedding happy in the certainty that we would go nowhere in the morning. The bride's father was a wealthy man; the reception was an enormous party at a large country club, and there were five open bars to service the huge crowd. After making the rounds of them all, then making the rounds again, I was having a great time dancing when it occurred to me that maybe Bob had cancelled the trip already, the weather still being ferocious; I found a phone booth and called him.

"I tried to call the group to cancel, but there wasn't any answer, so we have to show up at the boat," he replied to my query. "You'd better be on your feet," he added with a little cackle. But I was well past stopping.

I arrived at the boat on time but with the beginnings of a world-class hangover. Soon the customers, regular codfishermen, showed up with their coolers. They had no intention of calling off the trip if it was possible to go, and the wind had abated just a bit, so Bob agreed to go out and "take a look." We wound up getting the whole day in.

The trip out was total misery for me, shucking clams on the afterdeck, the quartering sea lifting and dropping the boat as we went. And then, sitting on anchor, the westerly current held the boat off the seas enough to make the deck both pitch and roll. During the day, Bob would say things to me like, "Man, the sea's right cranky today," or "Good thing you got enough work to keep your mind off your miseries," or "You gotta get those codfish guts off the deck, before somebody slips on 'em." But it was the ghost of a smirk and the slight twinkle in his eye that I found most aggravating.

My lowest point, the absolute nadir of my day, came in the early afternoon. The customers had gone into the deckhouse to grab a sandwich and a beer, and I was standing on deck, when a sudden wave of nausea swept over me. I looked at the horizon and breathed deeply, and it started to subside. But then came near-disaster. One of the customers was suddenly, ferociously, seasick. He ran out onto the deck and projectile vomited into the wind, upwind of where I was standing. That whole wad of vomit flew by my head while I was inhaling. My gorge rose as I turned away, eyes watering, cold sweat all over me, choking it back, gasping for air; in that instant I came very, very close to my only bout with sea-sickness.

I have always thought that the enormous differences in people's reactions to seasickness would make an interesting Ph.D. dissertation in comparative psychology. The man who vomited upwind of me that day accepted his friends' ballbusting with a smile—a forced smile, but a smile nonetheless—and went back into the deckhouse to finish his sandwich. "Gotta have something in my stomach, don't want the dry heaves," he said. This kind of stoicism is common in my blue-collar codfishing crowd. Even when laid out on a berth, head dangling in a bucket, retching deeply, they won't complain or suggest terminating the trip. The cynical might call this blue-collar heroics or macho behavior, but I don't think so. It is more an acceptance of things that can't be changed, the patience to ride out a bad time, and the understanding that, in the grand scheme of things, a bout of seasickness is a small cross to bear.

Then there are those who seem to really fear that their af-fliction is likely to be terminal. They slump to the deck, whimper-ing, and whine out pleas to be taken home or at least to the nearest shore. I can't help but feel a little contempt for this type, but I did say that I was deficient in empathy in the *mal de mer* department. Perhaps some people do get it worse than others do, but I doubt it. To me it seems selfish to insist that others terminate their fishing trips over one's personal discomfort.

Occasionally *mal de mer* stimulates practical jokes from those with a bit of a cruel streak. Once I was bluefishing with a group that included two fellows who were fighting nausea. They stood at the gunwale, looking at the horizon, breathing deeply. They were pale, but keeping it under control and enjoying the fishing during periods when it subsided, and I was sure they would be all right. But I didn't reckon with one of their friends. He was the type who slaps people on the back a lot and always seems to have too much to say and to say it too loudly. He came up to me, hit me on the back, and said, "Watch this." He filled his mouth with light coffee from a thermos, then ran to the gunwale between the two, pushed them aside and, with the most realistic retching sounds I have ever heard anyone perform, bent over the rail and blasted the café au lait out of his mouth. The response was instantaneous. His two victims both dropped to their knees, heads hanging over the side, and let it go. Their tormentor jumped to his feet and stood back, pointing at the two and belly-laughing. The victim on the right turned his head, eyes red and watering, and between spasms said, "You son-of-a-bitch, I'd kill you if I could move!"

Sometimes I run into people with the same lack of empathy that I have. A group of long-term regular customers, very serious anglers, but with one newcomer, arranged a trip for shark. We stopped five miles east of Block Island to catch a few bluefish for fresh bait. It was a choppy day, although not rough, and the newcomer soon became very seasick. Hanging over the gunwale, he kept looking at the island and begging to be taken there. We quickly got enough bluefish, and as I prepared to resume my course offshore, the leader of the group approached me, a look of painful concern in his eyes, and said, "Dave, Bill here is just awful sick, and I'm kind of worried. Why don't we just run him into the island before we head out?"

"That's fine with me," I replied, "but we're headed southeast, away from the island, and counting crossing the harbor and tying up, it'll take a half-hour each way."

"You mean an hour off the fishing?" he asked.

"Yep," I said.

His deeply concerned look instantly evaporated. "Screw him!" he said. "Let's go fishing!"

• • •

Over the last decade, a sea change has occurred in the American economy. I am most definitely not an economist, and I don't really understand all of what has happened, but its effects are evident in my charterboat business. Through the mid-1980s, more than 70 percent of my customers were blue-collar males who would probably be classified as lower middle class, and the most popular fish were cod, pollock, bluefish, and tautog. By the early 1990s this group was reduced to less than a quarter of my business and by the late 1990s to less than half of that. The far greater portion is now made up of doctors, dentists, lawyers, and middle-management people, along with an increasing number of women, and they prefer to go offshore for shark, tuna, and billfish. I have rarely gotten the truly wealthy because they generally have their own extravagant and very fast boats with hired crews and only book charters when visiting some exotic, usually tropical locale.

This change is not simply the result of a change in me or in the way I conduct my business. The charter captains who have deliberately targeted a working class clientele have steadily lost ground, and many have simply gone out of business. The same phenomenon has even affected the large head boats, which used to pack on people for low-cost bottom fishing. The head boats that have survived, and in many cases flourished, now also schedule much more expensive offshore and multi-day trips that require a reservation, and they set a limit to the number of people per trip. They still offer what are now called "open boat" trips, but they can no longer survive on that largely blue-collar trade alone.

What has changed? Far more than I would have believed possible a quarter-century ago. Charterboat fishing, defined simply as an individual or group hiring a boat with a guide to take them fishing, primarily for recreation, goes back a long way. George Washington chartered boats to go saltwater fishing on at least two recorded occasions, in Long Island and in New Hampshire. In New England, the tradition of commercial fishermen taking out parties from time to time to supplement their incomes survived the advent of full-time charter and party boats after World War I and didn't really end until quite recently. But end it did, in the economic and social upheavals that have ripped through all New England fishing ports over the past quarter century.

When I was a boy, commercial fishermen were hard-working family men who loved and respected the sea. Most were religious, and in many ports, such as New Bedford with its large Portuguese population, most of the boats would be home for Sunday church services and a family day. Drugs were unknown, and heavy drinking was rare and frowned upon. My father was a commercial fisherman back then, and although he wasn't a teetotaler, many of the men he fished with were, and even those who drank despised drunkenness and a man who couldn't "hold his liquor."

They also took great pride in both their seamanship and their mastery of the skills of fishing. The boats operated on shares, and a new man started as a quarter-share apprentice, only progressing to a half-share, three-quarter-share, and finally full share over a period of several years as he proved his proficiency to the skipper and the rest of the crew. Turnover was low, and the standards were high. A full-share man knew every piece of the boat from stem to stern, including the machinery, and could maintain it all. He could navigate with precision, read weather changes, make nets and repair them so perfectly that the repair wouldn't be visible, splice lines with tapers so perfect that they would slide unnoticed through a sheave, and tie any knot in an instant in total darkness; in a crisis he was decisive and didn't panic.

The charter captains of the same period were cut from the same cloth. Many started out as commercial fishermen and then built their own boats for chartering, either from scratch or from a commercial hull. During the winter some of them worked as transit men on draggers or lobster boats, filling in for regular crew taking time off, returning to chartering in the spring. The golden age for these men, the time that Captain Bob Linton called "the best of it," ran from the early thirties through the mid-seventies, with time out for World War II. Bob was the archetype, the quintessential charter captain, known and respected throughout the port, and the five years I worked for him on the MAKO II, a forty-three-foot offshore charterboat that he built with his own hands, were a graduate school in how to do it right.

What went wrong? Nowadays the commercial fleets, particularly the draggers, are riddled with crewmen who are drunks and drug addicts, while the ports are full of charterboats run by weekend wonders, and the two groups have, with few exceptions, nothing in common. What went wrong is that the fish stocks, which were the foundation of the old order, were destroyed. I have heard it said, by those trying to obfuscate and shift the blame, that it took generations to destroy the fisheries. That is a lie, although it is believed by many who are simply ignorant of what really happened and a few others who should know better. The plain fact is that it all happened in a very short time and for a very specific reason. The perpetrator was the U.S. Department of Commerce, its weapon was the subsidy and the loan guarantee, and the destruction took less than a decade for the demersal fish and a decade and a half for the pelagics.

These comments do not constitute a right-wing diatribe

against all government. There are certain essential functions of industrial and post-industrial societies that are best done by, and in many cases can only be done by, agencies of government within an open political process. We need look no farther than the National Weather Service to see a proper government role being effectively carried out. But there are many things that government cannot do well and still others in which government involvement invites disaster. Number one in this last category is the promotion and subsidization of particular industries, especially those based upon the extraction of common-property resources. When a government agency steps in to help "develop an underutilized resource" through subsidies and loan guarantees, the jackals and sharpies will be hard on its heels, and the resource will wind up endangered every time.

As the fish stocks were destroyed, the social fabric of the fishing communities unraveled. Desperation replaced dedication. Too many draggers started going too far and staying out too long, and people started to get hurt. The quality of the crews declined and then plummeted, and before long there were too many captains, hired by absentee owners, who wouldn't have been hired as full-share crewmen a generation earlier.

• • •

There was only a half-dozen men at the bar when I walk in, but it's early in the day and the fish plant is working for a change. Also, the weather was good so most of the boats was out. Or at least the ones the bank hasn't put padlocks on yet. I know all the guys, not all their names 'cause I ain't real good with names, but I know who they are. Some guys, I never know their names, but only know them by the boats they're on. Then there's guys like me that work a lot of boats, goin' transit when someone takes a trip off. I used to sometimes lump out boats for beer money, but I'm gettin' too old for that shit. Besides, most of the boats take out their fish with conveyors now anyways.

The bartender is that horse-faced shit Jack hired, Tom I think his name is, the one with the limp. I heard he come out of Stonington, worked on a boat down there until he got hurt. Someone said he got his foot wrapped up in the winch, busted all the bones. Anyways, I order up a rum and coke, and he don't say nothin' but just gives me that bum look of his. A couple a guys is playin' pool, so I go over and put a quarter on the table and play two or three games for drinks. Two more guys come in, and someone puts some money in the jukebox, then goes over and bitches to horse-face that it ain't loud enough.

I go back to the bar and get another drink, and I'm lookin' at the paper when this other guy comes in that I ain't seen before, but he looks like a fisherman. So he sits at the bar near me and orders a drink and just kind of looks around. After a while he says to me he's lookin' for a site, and he wants to know if anyone's hiring. Well, I just laugh at that one, the way things has been. I ask him where he comes from, and he says New Bedford and things are bad over there, too.

So we get to talkin', and he comes over to the next stool and says his name is Ed, and we shake hands, and I guess he hasn't worked in a while 'cause his hands isn't real hard. He buys another round and says the port looks pretty lively for things bein' so bad, so I tell him we had a pretty good shot of whiting and the price was good the last week or so what with it bein' Lent and all the weather so all the boys was out and the fish plant was workin'. I tell him I'm hopin' to get a trip in before things turn back to shit, and I see his eyes light up a little, so I say it won't last more'n another week and in this port you gotta know someone to get on a boat. Yeah, he says, I guess it's the same in every port. Well, you never know, I says, feelin' bad for the guy, ask around and you might just be in the right place at the right time.

He seems kind of down for such a young feller, but he buys us another round, and then he says he heard we lost a boat out of here a week or so ago. So I says yeah, hell of a thing, I knew all them guys. No shit! he says. Hell of a thing. I hear she got run down, tanker or somethin', they figure it out yet? Naw, I says, she was downside up when the chopper spotted her, but there was a sea on, and she sunk before the Coast Guard boats got there. No liferaft? he says. No EPIRB? Nothin'? Nothin', I says, and I'm thinkin about Dave and Jo-Jo and Jimmy and that kid, what's-his-name, that kid that was a lumper, on his first trip, and Big John with his black beard and that crazy big mustache of his that he waxed and pointed up on the ends, and all of them inside that boat layin' on the bottom of the ocean.

We say nothin' for a few minutes. Then he says, they musta got rammed by somethin' fuckin' big. Yeah, that's what was in the paper, I says. What else could it be, he says, goin' over so fast the fuckin' EPIRB didn't even get clear? I don't say nothin' right away 'cause I'm thinkin' about that night and what it was like and then I just says that I guess they go over real fast when they start to go.

Hell of a thing, he says, particularly when it's guys you know. Yeah, I says, and I'm thinkin' about Dave and Jo-Jo, who I knew real well, and Timmy the holdman who wasn't too bright but he was a happy-go-lucky shit and the new kid I didn't know except I seen him lumpin' and Big John, who everyone knew. So he asks me if she was one of the old eastern rig boats, and I tells him no, the OUTLAW was a steel hull with a western rig and a wide chute and real pretty lines and painted all black with the name in big white script letters on the side and a cowboy hat on the top of the O and crossed guns under it. Big John paid good money to get that done.

This shit gets a lot of 'em, he says, and he's holdin' his drink and lookin' into it. The OUTLAW was a dry boat, I says, no liquor aboard, I know 'cause I went transit on her a few times. Big John was the skipper, and he made that rule when they laid over in Stonington one time for repairs and John went up to Essex to get parts and he left the crew aboard overnight and they got stinkin' drunk and left the fuckin' deck hose hangin' over the side when they turned in. Course it back-siphoned through the pump and he had a four-inch hose on that boat, so when John came back the next mornin' the boat was layin' on the bottom. Good thing it was a low moon tide and the water didn't make it up to the main engine intake, but the generator was ruined and the reverse gear was full of water. I guess there was some ass-kickin' that day, I says. Hell, last year Big John fired a man for walkin' on the boat with a beer in his hand, and they wasn't even leavin' the dock that day.

So he says there's some of the old-timers over in New Bedford that's teetotalers, and I says John wasn't no teetotaler and if it was a storm he'd come in here and drink and he was real friendly when he had a couple and then when he had a couple more he'd go sit in the corner by himself and pretty soon there'd be tears comin' down his face but nobody bothered him, him bein' so damn big. He lost his wife and I guess he had a couple a kids but I don't know what become of them.

So then I says the only exception to the rule was the Blessin' of the Fleet, and they always done that up right. He kind of laughs at that one, and he says yeah, I guess that's a party in every port. Well, the OUTLAW done it up big time last year, I says; they filled up a fishpen with ice and beer and a couple hundred people come aboard and they run all around the harbor with flags and streamers and shit flyin' and throwin' cherry bombs and shootin' other boats with them paintball guns, man, they had a hell of a time. Then when it come their turn to parade by the bishop and get blessed, every damn person on that boat, men and women both, dropped their drawers all at once and mooned the bishop right there and about five thousand people watchin' and all the TV cameras, I says. But that old bishop was a cool one, he was, he never missed a beat with the holy water and he blesses all them bare asses and says the words and then he says it's nice to see the OUTLAW havin' such a good time and all them people laughed. They never showed it on the television though.

About then horse face comes over with fresh drinks, and he gives me his real shitty look and says they're on the boys across the bar, they come in earlier with a good trip of whiting. He looks at the guy next to me and says that I'm great at tellin' stories but they're mostly liquor. He's jokin' but it kind of pisses me off and I tell him to go fuck himself. He gives me another shitty look, and then he walks away.

So then this guy I'm drinkin' with, he says that Big John sounds like he was a hot shit, and I say yeah, he had a sense of humor all right. One time I was up to the sportin' goods store gettin' some paintballs and there's this monster shotgun in the rack so I says what the hell is that and the guy hands it to me and says double-barrel ten-gauge magnum made down in Brazil I think it was, and it's so fuckin' long and heavy I says I wouldn't want to tangle assholes with the man who shoots this thing, and the guy says well, you turn around 'cause he just come through the door, so I turns and it's Big John. So I says Big John, what in hell you plannin' to shoot with this cannon, and he says seagulls, I oughta be able to get two dozen per shot. And I says why, John, killin' seagulls is illegal, and he says I don't look upon it as killin' seagulls. I look upon it as feedin' fish.

We laugh a while over that one, and then I says no, they wasn't any angels. I says Big John didn't allow no drinkin' on the boat, but as soon as they got off, like most of the guys, like them guys over there, they'd head right up here to Jack's, or down the street to the Port O' Call. But they was sober when they was fishin', and they was god-damned good fishermen.

A few minutes later the guy says to me you don't figure she got hit, do you. No, I says, and nobody else does around here neither. How come the newspapers and the TV say she got rammed, he says. So I says that story come from Jack here, he owned half of her and I guess it's better for him that way. But it was a clear night, I says, and she wasn't in the shippin' lane. They said it mighta been a sub but that don't make sense neither 'cause they stay on the surface 'til they're off the shelf. No, I says, there was a sea on, and she filled up with water and rolled over. Well, that don't make sense neither, he says, 'cause they woulda felt her fillin' up. No, I says, they left at eleven and them boys was in here drinkin' 'til then. They was all asleep down below, and they woulda put the new kid on wheel watch and he woulda seen a ship comin' way off but he wouldn't have known enough to feel the boat fillin' 'til it was too late. She turned turtle with all them guys inside and no radio message and the EPIRB pinned under and no way to get to the raft and then she went down.

We don't say nothin' for a while and him lookin' at me and then he says holy shit real soft and then he says it again, and horse face is comin' over so I says to him two more and he says fuck you, Timmy, you had enough and you got a real big mouth and he's shoutin' the last of it. So I shout back what the fuck is your problem, and he looks at the other guy and says who the fuck is he, you don't know who he is, and I say he's just a guy from New Bedford, lookin' for a site and we're just bullshittin', and by now everyone's lookin' over at us and the guy says hey, I don't want no trouble here, I'll see you guys later, and he throws a couple a bucks on the bar and walks out. And horse face says to me you better get out, too. And I says fuck you, I gotta right to drink in here, and he says if Jack heard you he'd throw your ass out for good, now beat it, and I think about beltin' him in the mouth but I know he's got his hand on the baseball bat under the bar so I says fuck it and walks out.

When I get outside I see the guy from New Bedford up the street talkin' to some other guy in a suit and tie, and then I see the two of them get in a car, looks like a Buick or Olds, and drive off. I think about walkin' down along the docks but there ain't no one around now and the fish plant'll be lettin' out pretty soon and a lot of them guys will be goin' into the Port O' Call so I figure I'll walk on up there and get myself another drink and maybe shoot some more pool.

CHAPTER 4

Stripers and America; Learning Curve;
THE GOOD OLD DAYS; Epiphany

Nothing regarding [striped] bass is of greater interest to
commercial fishermen and to anglers than the great
fluctuations in its numbers that have taken place in our
Gulf within historic times.
—H. B. Bigelow and W. C. Schroeder,
Fishes of the Gulf of Maine, 1953

In a half-century on the ocean, nothing has made me happier
than the recovery of the striped bass. This response is more
emotional than intellectual. Sure, it is gratifying to see biology
and management work, but my reaction goes much deeper. Nearly
every charterboat captain in my area who is much over forty-five
first started serious fishing with stripers, either from a small boat
or from shore. The striper is the fish of our youth. After the seventies, when the stripers disappeared, we went on to other fish and
still had some grand times, but their loss left a hole, an underlying
sadness. There was a sense of youth irretrievably lost, a door to our
inner soul slammed shut. Getting the stripers back, when no one
really believed it would happen, was a rebirth, an affirmation of
our own continuity.

Stripers had been more than a fish; they were our source of

freedom. The freedom of solitude, of sunsets over the water with gulls crying in the distance, of beaches on cold nights with Orion blazing above, of sunrises with crashing surf and beating wings and throbbing life—of confronting the mysteries of existence and mortality. Back then we didn't really know where they came from or where they went, only that they returned every year in the spring and disappeared every year in the autumn and that it took years to really become an accomplished striper fisherman. We figured it was enough to learn the secrets of their haunts and the complications of their feeding without trying to figure out things like their breeding biology and migration routes.

Today it is much different. Back then we were apolitical loners, and the times passed us by as the resource was plundered under our nose in ways that we never understood. Today's angler is more politically active (or belongs to an organization that is) and informed. National and regional fishing magazines as well as outdoors columns in local newspapers regularly publish the results of scientific studies of striped bass (as well as other species), and the average angler is conversant in such subjects as Chesapeake fish, Hudson fish, spawning stock biomass, year class, sustainable yield, index of abundance, and so on. And yet, despite all that we know, the ancient mysteries remain. Even with modern fisheries science, I know of no one who, deep down, truly believes that we really understand the striped bass.

The striper's importance is hard to explain at the rational level. Stripers are not the easiest fish to catch, but they are also not the most difficult. They taste good and keep well, but others taste and keep better. They are a handsome fish, but others are prettier. Even their fighting ability is overrated. Yet the American angler (myself included) feels a special affection for them, and there have surely been more books written about striped bass than any other marine species. Looking through my own fishing library, I see that, although there has been no conscious bias on my part, books on the striped bass outnumber those on any other saltwater fish.

This emotional response to the striper is nothing new. Each generation has had its own special relationship to this fish, all the way back to Capt. John Smith and the very earliest settlers of the U.S. East Coast. Whether Pocahontas actually, in a fit of passion, saved Smith's life may be open to dispute, but his love of the New World is evident in his journal entries, which include this rather sensual description of the striped bass, written in 1614:

> They are so large, the head of one will give a good eater a dinner, & for daintinesse of diet they excell the Marybones of Beefe. There are such multitudes that I have seene stopped in the river close adjoining to my house with a sands at one tyde so many as will loade a ship of 100 tonnes. I myselfe at the turning of the tyde have seene such multitudes passe out of a pounde that it seemed to me that one mighte go over their backs drishod.

The early European settlement of New England apparently coincided with a period of great striped bass abundance. Twenty years after Smith's journal entry, in 1634, William Wood wrote the following in *New Englands Prospect:*

> Of these fishes some be three and four foote long, some bigger, some lesser; at some tides a man may catch a dozen or twenty of these in three hours. . . . When they used to tide in and out of the rivers and creekes the English at the top of an high water do crosse the creekes with long seanes or basse nets, which stop in the fish; and the water ebbing from them they are left on the dry ground, sometimes two or three thousand at a set, which are salted up against winter, or distributed to such as have present occasion either to spend them in their homes or use them for their grounds.

When Wood speaks of catching "a dozen or twenty of these in three hours" he is referring to his description of "taking a great cod line, to which he fasteneth a piece of lobster, and threwes it into the sea. The fish biting at it, he pulls her to him . . ." This method, handlining with a lobster tail as bait, continued in use for almost three centuries. When he says they would "use them for their grounds," he refers to the colonial practice of burying fish or fish parts as fertilizer, something I don't really understand, having once tried it with the result that raccoons, skunks, and cats tore up my garden. At any rate, there may have been a noticeable decline in bass abundance at about this time, because in 1639 the Massachusetts Bay Colony enacted a law prohibiting their use as fertilizer.

The following generation saw the striped bass as a means to civic improvement. In 1670 the Plymouth Colony enacted a law dedicating all income from their sale (as well as the sale of cod and mackerel) to the building of what became the first public school in colonial America. Salted and dried or pickled in barrels, the bass had become a staple of the colonial economy, and even with this harvest they appear to have continued in abundance through the remaining century of the colonial era. Then, during the years of America's War of Independence, there was a decline in their numbers all along the coast.

Through the early years of the nineteenth century their numbers again increased, and by 1829 heavy commercial catches were again being reported from New England. The population reached a peak around 1845, when there were so many stripers overwintering in Rhode Island's estuaries that large numbers were taken through the ice, and they remained abundant into the Civil War years. During this period a profound change was occurring in American society. The four decades preceding the Civil War were a bustling time of optimism, expansion, and economic growth. Prosperity came to the industrializing Northeast, Manifest Destiny expanded the western territories, and the population increased through immigration. The fishing reel was developed along with fine-diameter Irish linen fishing line, a sporting press emerged, and the people who comprised what historian Samuel Eliot Morison has called "this crucial generation, which in so many ways set the pattern of the America to come" began to look upon the striped bass as a sport fish.

After the Civil War American society became stratified, and for the first time in its history truly class-conscious. This was the era of the robber barons who amassed enormous wealth and came to see themselves as different from and superior to the rest of the human population—the product of what became known as social Darwinism. Much later this attitude was expressed in the widely reported but possibly apocryphal conversation between F. Scott Fitzgerald and Ernest Hemingway in which Fitzgerald stated his belief that "the wealthy really are different, Ernest." Hemingway, reflecting the older American way of thinking, simply replied, "Yes, they have money."

The relationship of the post-Civil War generation to the striped bass reflects its social stratification. The wealthy elite cruised the coast in huge and opulent yachts but, being basically landsmen, conducted their fishing from shore. They formed striped bass fishing clubs with very exclusive memberships, bought tracts of waterfront land along the rocky coast of southern New England, built large clubhouses that they lavishly supplied with food, good cigars, fine wines, and expensive liquors, and hired local people to do the work. The fishing was done from "stands" that extended outward from the south-facing shore for a hundred or more feet. These stands were made from wooden planks atop a frame of iron pipe drilled into the rock (today their rusted bases are a still-visible reminder of the ephemeral nature of human pretense).

The most famous of the exclusive striped bass clubs was the Cuttyhunk Club on Cuttyhunk Island, at the end of the Elizabeth Islands chain between the Massachusetts mainland and Martha's Vineyard. Formed in the last year of the Civil War, it counted among its fifty members magnates of the major industries of the day and among its guests only the wealthy and powerful, including at least one U.S. president. Many financial deals and political decisions were sealed in the club's parlor by portly men sitting in heavy leather-bound chairs sipping thirty-year-old brandy in front of a huge fieldstone fireplace.

The Cuttyhunk Club had twenty-six fishing stands, and the fishing day would begin in the early morning hours when each angler's chummer, usually a local fisherman, took a gunny sack of lobsters to his assigned stand and broke them up, saving the tails and scattering the rest as chum. Once the sun was well up, the angler (after a substantial breakfast) would stroll down to his stand, have his hook baited by his chummer, and make his first cast. The chummer would keep the angler's hook baited, gaff his fish, and carry everything back to the clubhouse at the end of the day. It was all very competitive, with a diamond-studded hook-shaped gold medal for the "high hook" and a bonus for his chummer.

Old photographs from the Cuttyhunk Club's glory days are poignant reminders of America's short flirtation with European-style castes. The anglers are ponderous men, finely dressed with gold watch chains hanging across large paunches, exuding arrogant self-importance both in stance and expression. The chummers are lean, hard men, tanned and wearing stout work clothes, exuding the strength and quiet competence of the Yankee fisherman. It is interesting to note that few of those fat rich men survived their sixties, while most of the Cuttyhunk fishermen lived in good health a quarter-century longer.

After 1895 club membership plummeted, although the club was not officially disbanded until 1922. Reasons that have been given for the fall include the death or physical infirmity of its members and the coming of the gasoline engine in small, able boats, making the stands obsolete. But the actual reason is revealed in the club's meticulously kept records: the coastal population of striped bass crashed, leaving the club bereft of a *raison d'être*. Along with balance sheets showing income and expenditures are found precise catch and effort records for most of the Cuttyhunk Club's existence—perhaps the most graphic, although unintended, picture there is of the steep decline of the striped bass in the last two decades of the nineteenth century. The club's best year was its first, 1865, when 1,252 fish were caught in a total of 556 fishing days. Success gradually tapered off and then plummeted after 1880, although a few trophy fish were still taken. After 1890 there was never a year when the total reached 100 fish, and after 1901 the catch was in single digits. After 1907 no one bothered to keep records, and the stands were allowed to deteriorate.

In his 1870 testimony before the special fisheries committee of the Rhode Island legislature, fisherman John Rice reported a sharp decline in all the species he fished for in Narragansett Bay, but he thought the problem was local and attributed it to excessive use of gillnets, standing fish traps, and seines. Further north, above Cape Cod, striped bass catches had already begun a noticeable decline by around 1862. During the 1870s this decline progressed steadily southward, and by the early 1880s the total coastal population had shrunk to a very low point. There was a somewhat successful breeding year in 1884, which supported a slight increase in catches into the beginning of the 1890s, but this temporary increase was followed by a population collapse that lasted more than a third of a century. By 1919 there wasn't a single striped bass reported from anywhere on the Massachusetts shore north of Cape Cod, and only 600 pounds were taken that year along the entire Maine coast. Striped bass fishing entered an eclipse, and by the time it reemerged the exclusive clubs were long gone and the elite class that had sustained them had been swept away.

Throughout this period the striped bass was in no danger of actual extinction, and occasionally someone would make a spectacular catch. In 1913 Charles Church of Cuttyhunk Island caught a seventy-three-pounder, within sight of the old club, which stood as the world record for decades, and there were a few years, particularly after 1921, when there was even a small commercial catch. But the huge schools of the colonial period and the mid-nineteenth century had vanished. They were gone from the beginning of the Gay Nineties through the Spanish-American War and the ascension of Teddy Roosevelt and the modern conservation movement. They were gone through the First World War and the Roaring Twenties. They were gone when the stock market collapsed along with the paper rich and when the country sank into depression, dislocation, and fear.

They finally returned—along with a New Deal and an old ideal. The bass came back in strength during the same time that egalitarianism was returning to American culture. In 1934 a very low breeding population produced an enormous spawn, which Bigelow and Schroeder in 1953 said "may prove a general rule." This explosion was followed by eight more years of successful breeding, five low years, and then a run of mostly good years that lasted for two decades and that profoundly affected post–World War II American culture.

This last statement may seem hyperbolic, but it really isn't. After the war, the striped bass spawned and shaped an industry and, more importantly, helped shape the attitudes of another crucial generation. Once their war was won, this generation returned to refashion their country (and, along the way, the world). They were optimistic and productive, a generation of doers whose opinions were shaped not by theory but by experience. War had taught them to live outdoors and to be mission oriented, and the excitement of chasing the striped bass in the wind and crashing surf of its natural environment was a perfect recreational outlet for their restless energy.

Soon there were hundreds and then thousands of new anglers ranging the coast in pursuit of the striper. Frank Woolner, who had fought his way across Europe in a tank, wrote columns and stories about stripers and teamed up with Henry Lyman, another war veteran, to create *Salt Water Sportsman* magazine, perhaps the greatest booster of the striper as everyman's sport fish. Their 1954 book, *The Complete Book of Striped Bass Fishing* (revised and reissued in 1983 as *Striped Bass Fishing*), was hugely popular and is still one of the best guides. Soon split bamboo poles and linen lines were supplanted as new companies designed fiberglass rods, synthetic lines, improved reels, and lures. The needs of striped bass anglers also dictated such innovations as new designs in rugged and able small boats with reliable motors, trailers, and vehicles to tow them. Soon the boom was shared by old seaside communities that had been depressed for years.

All this economic activity centered on the striped bass was important enough, but something more important was also happening. The crashing surf and lonely beaches, crying gulls and twittering shorebirds, clear water and salt air, clam chowder and hot coffee in seaside diners, driftwood fires on cold mornings, wild boat rides and thrill of the chase—all these elements cast their magic upon the soul of a generation. The baby boomers may like to take credit for the environmental movement that blossomed a quarter-century after the war, but all they really did was to plant seeds that would have come to naught had they not fallen on fertile ground. By the late sixties the war generation (the boomers' parents) controlled the media and held political and economic power at every level, and they were mostly receptive to the environmental message (although not always to the messenger). That receptivity, translated into a body of modern environmental law unprecedented in human history, was the result of their life experience—and for many, a part of that experience was fishing for the striped bass.

• • •

I first began fishing for stripers in the fifties. I would like to lie and say that I caught lots of big fish back then, but the fact is I didn't do very well. In 1953 my father bought a sweet eighteen-foot Thompson lapstrake boat with a twenty-five-horse outboard motor (the largest made then), and the next year he added a second motor. Since incurring an injury that had forced him out of commercial fishing and into a shore job, he never seemed to have the time to do much fishing, however, so I wandered the shore with an old fishing pole alone or with one or two friends. About 1957 I got a weekend job moving furniture for two old gals who owned an antique shop and saved enough from my sixty-five cents an hour to buy an eleven-foot Herter fiberglass surf-rod kit, the cheapest conventional reel that Penn made, and enough thirty-six-pound braided nylon line to almost fill it. I caught tautog from the rocks and fluke from a friend's skiff, but I couldn't afford much gear, and stripers still eluded me.

A year or so later I got a better job (a dollar an hour and regular hours) and bought a few good plugs, and by the autumn of 1959 I began to catch a few decent bass. But before I could really learn much, the Army, college, marriage, and babies got in the way. I returned to the coast on New Year's Day in 1967 and, except for short periods, have never since lived more than a couple of hundred yards from saltwater. I rebuilt the Herter rod for spinning, bought a new Mitchell 302 reel, and found that most of my new neighbors were striper fishermen. Over the next few years I caught stripers from shore and boat, in calm estuaries and on storm-wracked beaches, with live bait, rigged dead bait, and lures. I learned a lot about striped bass, although not enough even now to think I really know them, and as I write this chapter, so many years later, the old Herter rod, rebuilt for the umpteenth time this past winter and sporting another new reel, sits on the wall next to me. I pretty much retired it toward the end of the seventies when the stripers disappeared, but now that they are back I am using it again, although it has taken a permanent set and I try to go easy with it.

• • •

We all have a few days in our lives that stand out in memory—days that shine brightly while we are living them and then recede into the past with a burnished glow, not really faded and readily accessible throughout the remainder of our lives. Later experiences may change our perception of a particular golden day, tinting it with joy, with sadness, even with a bit of remorse, but its glow remains.

One of my golden memories is of a striped bass trip I took with two old friends, Billy and George, in early November 1968. Billy's father was a merchant mariner, and after high school Billy attended the Maine Maritime Academy, graduated as a third engineer, and went to sea. He soon made second engineer, and when the Vietnam War heated up, he volunteered for the munitions run, made first engineer, and began to rake in the money. When he was home, Billy played the hard-living seaman's role well—spending money, buying toys, chasing women, and partying. I can still see Billy at sunrise after an all-nighter, bleary eyed, sitting at the kitchen counter of the lakefront cottage he had bought with cash after the payoff from a trip, a beer and a cigarette in one hand and a fork in the other, eating a plate of scrambled eggs (he must have fried up a half-dozen), forkfuls alternating with pulls on the beer and the cigarette; and on another day, at an afternoon beach party, me with the girl who would become my first wife, Billy with a girl from the university who had what in those days was called a fast reputation, and then Billy and the girl wandering off into the dunes, Billy suddenly reappearing with a towel gathered around him, breathless and wild eyed, "Anybody got a rubber? It's an *emergency,*" someone tossing him one, Billy turning and dashing back into the dunes.

George was a big Swede, born three days later than me and in the same hospital. George was quiet and introspective, although every so often he would sort of explode. One year during high school a bunch of us camped out by a trout stream on the night before opening day, but George couldn't be there because he had to work. After work he got a sailor to buy him a pint of rum, and about two o'clock in the morning he came running through our camp, swinging a machete, screaming like a banshee, and cut every line, dumping the tents on top of the sleeping campers. George and I were in the same class, but we didn't graduate together, because five weeks before graduation George suddenly lit out for the West Coast and enlisted in the Navy when he got to San Diego. We were discharged from the service at about the same time, George from the Navy and I from the Army, and we rented a house together while we went to college, dirt poor, living like rats. We bummed across the country a couple of times, and once, hiking in the mountains of Wyoming, I took a bad fall and broke a hip and big squarehead George dragged my sorry butt out. George loved two things, marine biology and art. He walked the shore a lot, poking around in tide pools and turning over rocks, and he did fine oils, although they were mostly of dark, lonely beaches and people to match.

In the autumn of 1968 Billy was home from the bomb run for a couple of months, George was working a factory night shift and trying to make it as an artist, and I had been married for three years and had two little boys. Narragansett Bay was full of stripers and bluefish, and we had been doing pretty well fishing from shore. But Billy figured he could do a lot better from a boat, so he bought a twenty-one footer with a cuddy cabin and a huge outboard motor from a guy whose wife had just left him and tied it to a mooring off the beach at Jamestown. That evening he and his dad took a trial run and found the bass thick in the open water off Taylor Point. All excited, he called George and then he called me, and we set it up to go the next morning.

At the beach it was still dark; the breeze had come northeast and the weather looked ugly. Even in the harbor there was a little chop, and it took three trips in the tiny dinghy to get the three of us with all our stuff out to the boat. Billy rowed out with me, I rowed back and got a load of gear, then I rowed back again and got George. By the last trip there was just enough light to look over Billy's new boat. Actually, it wasn't all that new. It was wood, lapstrake, kind of boxy and high sided, a design that was popular in the fifties, and I judged it to be about ten or twelve years old. I also figured it to be a pounder in a choppy head sea. The motor was only a couple of years old, the massive high-horsepower sort of machine that was typical of the sixties.

The wind was coming on more as we ran from the harbor area into the more open bay, and Billy had to slow way down as he turned into the sea, although the boat had an easier entry and pounded a lot less than I had expected. Spray flew up onto the windshield, and George said, "Taylor Point's not gonna be any good." Taylor Point points north-northeast, right into the now clearly increasing wind.

"Yeah, but it's been loaded with fish there," Billy answered.

"New boat," George said. "Engine quits, you're fucked. Be on the rocks before you can do anything."

Billy was still jogging into it, looking straight ahead with his eyes bright like they sometimes got. The boat was lifting and plunging, and we weren't even to the new bridge yet.

"Been a lot of fish around Mackerel Cove, Billy," I said. "We can work Kettle Bottom Rock over to Short Point and be out of the shit."

Billy thought it through, and then he turned and looked downsea. The weather was getting worse, and even going to Mackerel Cove it wouldn't be any picnic coming home. "Yeah, let's give that a shot," he finally said, bringing the boat around.

Billy powered up to match the speed of the sea, and we ran in the trough, straight and level, and drank hot coffee from my big thermos, all the way to the calm water in the lee of old Fort Wetherill. We strung our rods and put on Danny plugs and Rebel swimmers and started to work the rocks to the west. By the time we got to Kettle Bottom there was a spitting, cold drizzle, and the wind coming off the shore was too much to cast into with the plugs, so we switched to Kastmasters and bucktails.

Kettle Bottom Rock is actually a reef made up of several rocks. It sits a couple of hundred yards out from the east side of Mackerel Cove's mouth, which faces south toward the open ocean. Although protected from the northeast wind, in heavy southerly weather the sea breaks over the rocks and baitfish get trapped behind them, easy pickings for striped bass. We drifted along outside of the reef, casting in among the rocks, when the fish suddenly erupted on the other side.

"Jesus Christ, look at that!" Billy yelled, dropping his rod and jumping to the helm. Blue smoke pluming from the outboard, the stern digging in, we flew out of the hole and around the end of the reef, my bright Kastmaster bouncing in the wake as I cranked to bring it in. Billy slowed and circled the fish, now breaking all across the open water between Kettle Bottom and the shore, gulls already working and more coming on a beeline, and then he stopped the boat on their upwind side. "Bet it's just bluefish, but hey!"

I shot a quick cast, began to retrieve, hooked a fish, lost it. "I don't think so, Billy. That one didn't hit like a blue, hit more like a bass," I said.

George cast, hooked up, and the fish sounded. "I think it's a bass," he said.

Billy jumped up on the foredeck, shot a hard cast, and cranked the lure back fast and near the surface. Nothing happened. He switched to a heavy bucktail, lobbed it out, let it sink a few feet, began a slower, jigging retrieve, and hooked up. George had his fish up almost to the boat, so I set my rod aside and picked up the net. The water was dark and turbid, but I saw the fish flash white. *"Bass!"* I shouted. *"A nice fish!"*

It was a nice fish, although smaller than it had seemed in the water, thirty inches on the scale and maybe fourteen pounds. Billy's fish looked like it came from the same cookie cutter, and I got one, and George got another before the wind pushed us out of them. Over the next couple of hours they kept feeding, and we made drift after drift, the only boat around, as the wind gusted and slowly increased and the spitting drizzle got steadier. By the time the frenzy ended, the fishbox was full of striped bass, and we were releasing them. They were all the same size but one. I tangled my line on one cast and stopped to clear it, letting the lure sink. When I got it clear and started to retrieve, the lure was hung up. "Shit, I'm on the bottom," I said. But it wasn't the bottom, and a few minutes later George slid the net under a thirty-pounder.

It ended suddenly, as these frenzies always do, although we were still fired up. There were no fish in sight, and the gulls had settled down on the rocks and in the water. "It's all over," I said.

"Yeah, but they're still around here somewhere," Billy said. "Maybe we can find them."

But we didn't. We trolled down the shore with tandem worm rigs, plugs, and rigged eels, casting the heavy metal spoons into likely looking spots, and never had a touch from a bass. When we got even with Short Point a trolling rod went down, but it was a mackerel. The ride back was nasty, particularly the last mile before the harbor, and my teeth were chattering when we reached the mooring. It took several trips with the dinghy, ferrying gear and fish, bailing as the chop slopped over the side, to get us all ashore. We drank beer and cleaned fish on the table in Billy's backyard, laughing and shivering, by now wet through. My wife showed up with dry clothes, then one of Billy's girlfriends showed up, and we ended the day in front of a fire sipping bourbon, the wind and rain now lashing the side of the house.

A couple of years later Billy married a girl from New York and left the sea, as he had always said he would. He bought an old hotel with a restaurant that looked out over the water and a long oak bar in a separate room with a massive fieldstone fireplace, and a bunch of us got together to help him clean and paint the whole place. He hired a chef from Boston and got off to a good start. It was a great party for a couple of years, but Billy wasn't much of a businessman, and the place sucked up everything he had accumulated, and he finally had to sell out to a developer who turned it into condominiums. Billy had to go back out to sea, and somewhere along the line his wife left him and took their child, and the last time I saw Billy it was a warm spring morning and he was chain smoking and drinking beer. On another morning in the summer he was fifty-one, Billy had a massive heart attack and was dead before he hit the floor.

George sold a few paintings and quit the factory, but then he started to drink a lot. He was a quiet drunk and never got into fights, but he ran his car off the road a couple of times and his output of paintings went way down. He got a job working nights in a liquor store and moved into an apartment by himself. As the years passed he became increasingly reclusive, and one by one, his old friends gave up on him. He didn't have a phone and never answered the doorbell, so I stopped in at the liquor store one night, but he was like a stranger, and we didn't have anything to talk about. We agreed to get together, but we never did. Just after his forty-eighth birthday, George went home from work one night and killed himself. No one even knew he owned a gun.

I guess all of us drank too much back then. With me drinking was just one more way that I didn't control my appetites. I drank and got drunk the same way that I ate and got stuffed on Thanksgiving or the way that I overindulged in sex between my marriages. I enjoyed the hell out of it, but I never craved a drink. I let it go when I got older and hangovers became a real pain, although once in a while I still let the dog out of the cage.

I think it was the same with Billy, at least in the beginning. He slammed into life the way that I did, only more so. It wasn't that we were carefree but that we were careless. We didn't want to hurt anyone, but people around us got hurt. Toward the end—I don't know. Maybe the booze got him, but I don't think that was exactly it.

With George it was different. If alcoholism is, in fact, a disease, then George had it. There was a cold desperation about his drinking, something I didn't understand until it was way too late, and it was what turned the man who saved me in the mountains into someone I didn't know, years later, in a small-town liquor store.

I wonder if things could have turned out differently. Maybe with a little more effort we could have stayed closer and had more good days. We all have dark places in our souls into which the golden days of memory shine a bit of light. But I guess for my two old friends the darkness was too deep, the light of good days not bright enough or well enough remembered.

• • •

The striped bass had a good breeding year in 1970, and commercial landings peaked in 1973. From that point, there was a steady decline through the rest of the decade, by the end of which the population had again collapsed, as it had almost a century before. I gave up on the species and would neither book a striper charter nor waste time fishing for them myself. Considering the overall rape of ocean resources, I had little hope of seeing them return in my lifetime. I told them goodbye and closed the books on a part of me.

It seems likely that the collapse was mostly caused by the overharvest of juvenile fish, mostly by Chesapeake Bay commercial fishermen, although that supposition is open to argument. Salinity changes from yearly variations in freshwater runoff, and pollution may also have been involved. Also uncertain is why, in the midst of a string of disastrous spawning years, 1982 was moderately successful. To the credit of everyone involved and in a model of how things should be done but almost never are, tight controls were placed on the fishery by every coastal state from Virginia to

Maine with the intention of preserving this single year class until they could successfully spawn. And it worked.

After 1987 there was a run of good spawning years overall, although not in every area. Then came the explosion that was 1993, with high yield throughout all of the striper's regular breeding areas. By the time the figures were in, 1993 was among the best spawning years ever recorded for the striped bass. The following year, several Chesapeake watermen told me that there were so many juvenile stripers that the bottom seemed paved with them, and they were catching them in their oyster tongs. "When them fish get up to your country," one told me, "y'all are gonna be *walkin'* on 'em."

Actually, our striper fishing began to show some feeble signs of improvement at the very end of the eighties, and I began to fish for them myself occasionally, although I didn't think it was good enough to begin booking striper charters. As the nineties began, the improvement picked up steam, and the variety of sizes being seen made it evident that there had been several successive good year classes. But the pessimism of a decade was hard to overcome. There was a part of me that didn't trust the widely hailed but nascent striped bass recovery.

My mind was changed one day in August 1992. My charter arrived late for a tuna trip and decided to convert to inshore, first trying for striped bass and then settling in for some light-tackle bluefishing. By the time we got under way the sun was bright in the sky and the tide wasn't really right for stripers, but they wanted them so badly that I headed for one of the reefs off Block Island to give it a shot. When we got there I put out a pair of pork-rind sweetened jigs at the end of two hundred feet of wire line and showed the anglers how to work them. I then went forward to the helm and watched the fishfinder as we came up onto the reef.

Right at the edge in forty feet of water I marked a huge pile of fish that showed a blob of yellow with red spots scattered through it. It rose from the bottom to within fifteen feet of the surface—no question about this, or so I thought. "Bluefish," I yelled back. "Hang on, you're both gonna get hit!" And sure enough, both rods went down. I was wondering how long my two bottles of pork rinds would last in the chopping teeth of a bluefish blitz when one of the anglers yelled out, "This is awful heavy for a bluefish!" Both rods were deeply bent, and the lines were going out. "We get some real alligators here—just keep the pressure on," I said.

But my first doubts started when the fish stayed deep and wouldn't budge. And I knew I had been totally wrong even before I saw the white bodies, the huge girth, and finally the dark stripes. I slipped the landing net under first one, then the other—fat striped bass, one around thirty pounds and the other almost forty.

For me it was a defining moment. Here I was on a calm day in bright sunlight with the tide all wrong and an enormous pile of stripers under me who were anxious to feed. Right then and there I thought about all the tiny bass in the estuaries and all the schoolies in the salt ponds and all the large bass we were live-lining on the reefs at night—and a great big smile welled up from deep inside of me. The bass really were back. Since then the bass and those of us who fish them have had more good years, and although I don't trust the science and I am not sure anyone really knows why the stripers are solidly back, I am confident that their return is sustained.

For those of us on the far side of fifty who have seen so much lost, the striped bass recovery means more than the return of a fish and fine days and nights on the water. It also means a return of something important in our youth that had been lost. And it also represents something far more important—a return of optimism, a hope for the future. For if we can get back the striped bass, there is no reason to accept the loss of any fish.

CHAPTER 5

Squeteague, Pollock, and How to Deplete a Resource

Thousands upon thousands of fish were caught, shimmering in the moonlight as whole families walked into the sea to collect them from the nets.
Now the great trawlers had taken toll the fish came less. It was wistful to watch the men waiting: even on the boats.
—Sven Berlin, *Jonah's Dream,* 1964

Squeteague *(Cynoscion regalis)* are truly beautiful fish. They have mossy green backs with darker spots grading to coppery gold sides, and they glint and flash in the sun. Squeteague have also been called sea trout, or spotted sea trout, from their superficial resemblance in color and marking to freshwater trout, although the two are not related. A much more common name is weakfish, by which they are known along much of the Atlantic coast. This name supposedly refers to a rather light-duty jaw structure and the fact that if you try to horse them in they often break off. But I dislike the negative connotation of a name like weakfish for such a lovely animal; I prefer the older and more romantic Indian name and use it exclusively.

I didn't really discover squeteague fishing until I was in my twenties and had a young wife and two little sons. We lived on Narragansett Bay in an area called Hamilton Beach, a small community of winterized beach houses that were mostly rented to poor young families or students. I worked the second shift in a factory, where I learned the machinist trade, and was a part-time college student during the day.

I also ran a short string of lobster pots, tonged for hard clams (quahogs), and caught fish with the old Herter fiberglass surf rod that I had converted to spinning and equipped with an inexpensive reel. My boat was something to behold. I couldn't afford much, but resourcefulness is often an attribute of youth and poverty. It was a sixteen-foot, flat-bottom, wooden bay skiff that had been given to me by a commercial quahogger who lived down the street and wanted it out of his backyard. The sides were sound, but the bottom was rotted and had a large hole punched through it. I went to work on the old boat with more optimism than skill, replacing the bottom with plywood and repainting the whole thing, finally adding a fierce-looking eye on each side just back from the stem. I wanted also to paint on a mouth with big, sharp teeth in the manner of the Flying Tiger fighter planes of World War II, but my artistic skills were not equal to the task.

I bought an equally old fifteen-horsepower Evinrude outboard for twenty dollars, payable if I could get it started. It had been sitting in a basement for some years without being serviced properly, and both of its pistons had seized up. I brought it home, soaked the outside with penetrating oil, and slowly removed the spark plugs and the head. The tops of the pistons didn't look too heavily corroded, so I poured in CRC, left it a few days, and started tapping on them with a hammer and a hardwood dowel. It took more than a week of tapping, soaking, tapping, and soaking before the pistons started to move and another week before they moved freely. I changed the oil in the lower unit, put it all back together, suspended it from a two-by-four across the top of a garbage can filled with water, and tried to start it.

On the second pull the rotted rope broke, so I jerry-rigged a piece of clothesline and tried again, but after a half-hour nothing had happened. I determined that there was no spark, so chased around the local marinas until I found a magneto that would fit. Now I had spark, but the motor still wouldn't start. I tried squirting a little ether into the cylinders. It would catch and then quit, so I took the carburetor apart, cleaned every bit of it with naphtha and a toothbrush, and put it back together. This time, on the fourth pull, it caught, ran a moment, and quit. After I repeated the steps a few more times, it finally caught, ran roughly for a few moments, and then smoothed out. It was raining that day, and I stood there soaked, rain streaming down my face, holding the handle of that purring little motor and feeling like a million dollars. The next day I paid the twenty dollars, and over the years I had the old Evinrude motor it needed no further repair and never once quit or let me down.

The boat, however, was another story. In my happy ignorance I hadn't fastened the bottom properly, and besides, the plank-bottom bay skiffs of that period weren't designed to use plywood. The old boat was sturdy enough, but it always leaked. I made a mooring by dragging an old Chevy engine block into the water off the little beach at the end of our street (you could still do that in the sixties). One end of a piece of chain was threaded through its front cylinder and the other was tied to a length of stout rope with three plastic bleach bottle floats tied to its far end so I could find it. But then I discovered I couldn't leave the boat tied off to the mooring because it would sink, so I wound up simply dragging it up onto the beach and leaving it there. I don't believe there was ever any danger that anyone would steal it. Now I was a bona-fide Narragansett Bay waterman.

I had some fine years with that little underpowered skiff. I ran my lobster pots, tonged for quahogs, and fished for striped bass, flounder, and tautog. I learned many of life's lessons with that boat, and it introduced my young sons to the water. Later I used it to start the research that became my master's thesis. And along the way I discovered fishing for squeteague.

I was aware of squeteague, of course, and had caught them occasionally while fishing for summer flounder along the ocean-facing beaches. But the big squeteague run, when you could go out and specifically target them, occurred in Narragansett Bay during early May, a time when there is always too much else that needs doing. For many of my friends, though, fishing the spring squeteague run was an annual ritual, so it was inevitable that, sooner or later, I would give it a try.

One fine May morning in the late sixties I did just that. It was clear and chilly, and the stars were fading in the eastern sky as I attached the outboard to the transom, packed my tackle and lunch aboard, and dragged the boat to the water. I also brought along my tongs, reasoning that if the fishing wasn't all it was cracked up to be, at least I could try out some new quahogging spots. There was no wind, and the bay was glassy as I crossed the cove inside of Rome Point and passed the rocks called the Seven Sisters, where the bass fed at night. I put up rafts of gulls crossing the channel, my wake forming a clean V behind, the reddening sky reflected in the water's smooth surface before me.

I passed Fox Island and dozens of lobster pot markers, some of which were mine, and headed north, up the bay, past Quonset Point and the enormous old aircraft carrier USS WASP, then in the last years of her career. It was only ten miles to the mouth of Greenwich Bay, the hot spot for the earliest part of the squeteague run, but it took my boat the better part of an hour to get there, and the sun was well up when I stopped in the deeper water outside of Hunt Ledge and tied on a small leadhead jig for my first drift on the ebbing tide.

Three hours later the tide was slack, and other than losing a couple of jigs on the bottom, absolutely nothing had happened. The warm sun and lack of action had sapped my enthusiasm along with my energy, and I was sprawled on one of the bench seats, my legs over the side, bare feet dipping into the chilly water with each rocking of the boat, fishing rod held slackly across my belly. Except for the necessity of occasionally bailing out the boat I probably would have gone to sleep.

Slowly the tide turned and began to flood, and I let the boat just drift along with it, having decided that either the squeteague were a fishermen's myth or their migration was behind schedule. Still in the deeper water I drifted slowly inward, past Round Rock and the buoy just north of Sandy Point, then on the quickening tide into the shallower water east of Sally Rock Point. I sat up and looked over the side, beds of eelgrass now clearly visible on the bottom, and reeled my jig up a bit. And that, as anyone who knows squeteague will have already guessed, is when it happened.

At first I thought I had hung up on the bottom, and then, when the throbbing told me it was a fish, I thought it must be a really early summer flounder. But it was a squeteague, and a good one, a fish of about ten pounds. I brought him aboard with a gaffhook and dispatched him with a fish billy. He lay in the bottom of the boat, sides flashing gold in the bright sun, and I knew he was the most beautiful fish I had ever seen. I lifted my squeteague and looked at him from every angle, then dressed him out. His stomach was full of grass shrimp, so I started the motor and slowly moved back to the edge of the eelgrass, where the grass shrimp live, and drifted back over it again. Two drifts brought two more squeteague, but by then I was out of time and had to leave to make my afternoon shift at the factory.

What I had discovered that morning about squeteague was reinforced by later experience. Squeteague are a schooling fish, prefer a sandy or grass-covered bottom, and are not usually found in water much deeper than about forty feet. Even when they migrate they stay in shallow water, hugging the coast as they move, making them very vulnerable to pound nets or gillnets strung from the shore. Years after my first experience with them I worked on a charterboat in the port of Galilee, tied up next to the lobster boat docks. By that time, many of the lobstermen owned lightweight monofilament gillnets that they set in the morning before working their lobster traps and pulled in the afternoon on their way in. The fish buyers would meet them at the dock with refrigerated trucks. Day after day I saw the buyers fill their trucks with boxes of squeteague for shipment to New York. The fishermen would often string their nets from the shore straight out, and I doubt that many squeteague made it through the gauntlet. After a couple of years the Narragansett Bay squeteague simply disappeared, and since then, although there have been many fine May mornings, I have never returned to the eelgrass beds inside Sandy Point.

● ● ●

It is no longer legal to set gillnets from shore and hasn't been for years, but the squeteague have never really returned. The stocks are supposedly recovering, but catches are sporadic, and no one has seen them in anything like the numbers we once had. The last time I saw a large body of squeteague in our waters was in early July 1984, and it wasn't in Narragansett Bay, but on the sandy shoal north of Block Island. Their presence was openly reported on the radio, so by the time I arrived at least fifty boats were lined up, drifting on the ebb tide across the shoal, catching a mixture of squeteague and bluefish on small jigs, then running to the top of the line of boats to drift down again. In the deep water just west of the shoal a small dragger, whose captain was a friend of mine, was towing his net for flounder. I had a bluefish charter aboard, and although I don't like fishing in crowds, I figured that a few squeteague would be a nice bonus, so I went to the head of the line and set in.

I quickly became frustrated. Jigging isn't difficult, but there is a bit of a knack to it, and my people couldn't quite get it. They caught bluefish, but only an occasional squeteague, while the local anglers in other boats were catching two or three on every drift. I tried my best to explain the technique, but I could tell by their expressions that in their eyes the fault was mine. The last straw was when one of the other boats came up alongside and one of its occupants, a man whom I vaguely knew, yelled out to me, "That draggerman's an asshole!"

"How come?" I yelled back.

"He'll grab all these squeteague!"

"No way," I yelled. "He's towing in ninety feet of water. He's working on flounder!"

"Bullshit!" He yelled back. "These fish are worth a lot of money, and he came over here to grab 'em! Couple of the guys already went over and threw sinkers at him!"

I had had enough and more. I took my charter south of the island, where there were plenty of bluefish, but no squeteague.

The following July there were scattered rumors of squeteague in that same spot, but I never heard it reliably substantiated. Since then I haven't seen any, nor have I heard of any caught there.

Why haven't the squeteagues returned? Their near-shore, shallow-water lifestyle has made them vulnerable to assault from many different directions. During the good years, the annual commercial catch averaged around 40 million pounds and made up three-quarters of the harvest. By 1980, the recreational catch had risen a bit higher than 40 million, or a bit over half the total catch. But at the same time pollution was rising in the squeteague's mid-Atlantic tidewater spawning grounds, and there was never a good spawning year class after 1978. In addition, the reduced number of juveniles that have been produced have been largely destroyed in their first and second years by North Carolina shrimp trawlers. And there is still no effective plan by the National Marine Fisheries Service to bring about their recovery. While squeteague are fecund and may have been able to withstand a single assault, the combination has all but wiped them out along the entire Atlantic coast.

• • •

New England's salt marshes and estuaries are her most biologically productive habitats. The flows of the tides import nutrients, minerals, and oxygen-rich water, and the ebbs export excess biomass (both living and dead) and wastes, while the sun on the flat, open terrain provides a steady energy source to drive the living systems. So much energy is captured and stored by the photosynthetic grasses and algaes that it builds up in the accumulating salt-marsh peat, and the very muck is alive with thousands of species of bacteria, worms, molluscs, echinoderms, and arthropods.

During winter, the low angle of the sun keeps the energy flux low, and many of the living biota lie dormant. But at the approach of the vernal equinox, as the sun charges northward, salt-marsh grasses turn green and salt-pond mud darkens with new life. Algae bloom, crabs scurry about, insects hatch, small fish feed along the water edges, flounder emerge from the mud and spawn, redwing blackbirds arrive and sing the boundaries of their territories, and above it all ospreys circle and watch for the careless.

From somewhere out to sea, hordes of harbor pollock *(Pollachius virens)*, eight to sixteen inches long and one or two years old, migrate to the estuaries to feed on copepods and small fish, part of the excess production swept out from newly active salt marshes. Or, rather, the pollock used to arrive in hordes. During the sixties and seventies harbor pollock swarmed through the seawall openings and into Point Judith Pond (actually an estuary) in early April, about two weeks ahead of the first schools of small striped bass. As they crossed the East Ground off Block Island the charter captains on cod trips often cursed them as bait-stealers, sometimes even worse than the ubiquitous cunners. Then, toward the end of the seventies, the little pollock simply disappeared, at least south of Cape Cod. Overfishing of the spawning stock certainly played a role, perhaps the major role, but the story of the pollock is more complex than that of the squeteague.

For several more years after the disappearance of the in-shore run of juvenile pollock we could still fish for jumbos, some over forty pounds, on the humps south of Block Island. These fish came in behind huge schools of sand eels (also called the sand lance, *Ammodytes americanus*) in early May, which they gorged upon until rising water temperature drove them out in mid-June. Popular wisdom holds that the jumbo pollock left our waters with the apparently cyclic decline of the sand eels. But the sand eel decline didn't occur until the end of the eighties, and the last good jumbo pollock year was 1984.

Harbor pollock, along with tinker mackerel and skipjack bluefish, were once considered a kid's fish, caught from piers and docks on cheap tackle and little flashy lures or pieces of bait on small hooks. But in my mind they will always be linked to a time of personal turmoil. In that long-ago memory it was a fine spring day in early April, but my own life was a shambles, and I was heartsick and confused by impending loss and the need to make a hard decision. It would be a choice not, as John Steinbeck once said, between "good and bad, but between bad and worse," the kind of choice that, once made, you learn to live with but look back upon many years later and wonder how things would have turned out if you had gone the other way.

But the decision hadn't yet been made or even yet squarely faced, which is probably what drove me to the edge of the sea. I tossed a spinning rod and a small box of lures into the back of my station wagon and drove south along the shore. I stopped in a little restaurant in the fishing village of Galilee, sat by the window, looked out into the bright sunlight, ate clam cakes and hot chowder and drank a beer while I watched a dragger come through the west gap of the seawall into the Harbor of Refuge and slowly move up the channel. She was in from an offshore trip, loaded and low in the water, and I watched her tie up to the pier in front of me, the crew laughing and horsing around. I left the restaurant and drove around to the east end of the seawall, right at Point Judith, and walked out on its huge boulders, my fishing rod in one hand and the box of lures in the other, until I came to the east gap, a half-mile out, the ocean on my left and the protected Harbor of Refuge on my right.

As I walked atop the giant boulders I tied a weighted spoon onto my line and made occasional casts, first to one side and then to the other. It was a half-hearted effort, and I suppose that, had I been asked, I would have said I was checking for an early striped bass. I know that is what was in my mind when I reached the gap, cast out into the channel, began a slow, jerky retrieve, and almost immediately hooked up a fish. There was no real weight, but the fish was scrappy, and for the first time in months I felt my heart lift as he zipped from side to side and up and down. I was thinking schoolie striper, but when I swung him up on the rocks he was a pollock—pointed nose, dark green on top, buttery yellow below, white lateral line, and about fifteen inches long.

I cut off a piece of line and strung the fish on it, then climbed down the rocks and rinsed my hands in the cold, clear water. Kneeling there, I watched rockweed swaying back and forth in the surge of the current, tiny killifish swimming through the fronds. I looked up, and suddenly I saw bright sunlight sparkling on the water, the misty cliffs of Block Island across the sound, white gulls against dark rocks, a yellow slicker-clad lobsterman hauling his pots a half-mile off the point, a red tug bound for New York, its diesel engine a distant throb. My pain didn't go away, but at that moment I knew that I would survive it.

• • •

My life's crises seem to have always driven me to the ocean. A decade later, facing another upheaval, I quit my job as a fisheries biologist (no great loss—the politics of a state agency had become too stifling to a still-young idealist) and went fishing as the mate on a charterboat. On spring cod trips if the wind was northeast and the sea too nasty to make the run to Cox Ledge, we would fish for smaller cod on the lumps south of Block Island. By early May, as schools of jumbo pollock moved in, we could always make a few drifts over them and catch several on jigs, a nice bonus for a cod charter disappointed at being unable to fish the Ledge. Then, in the late seventies, we discovered downriggers.

The first Point Judith charter captain to use downriggers was Mario Pagano, and I remember the ballbusting he had to endure the first year. They looked like two small cannons on either corner of his transom. When he entered a bluefishing fleet, as the mate was attaching the round ten-pound lead "cannon" balls to the "muzzle" end, someone would always get on the radio and say something like, "Scatter, boys, before he opens fire!" But Mario was onto something because, unless you had an experienced mate, the downriggers proved clearly superior to our old standard wire line for most bluefish trolling.

Since experienced mates were in short supply, within a year Mario had been vindicated, and virtually every charterboat had installed the new downriggers. The few experienced mates then developed ways of using both wire and downriggers together, adding new efficiency to the slaughter of bluefish. Along the way, someone thought of using them on the spring run of jumbo pollock. The first attempts were not particularly successful, the pollock proving more skittish than bluefish, but soon a method evolved that was truly deadly.

Most of the pollock concentrated to the west of Shark Ledge, holding with schools of sand eels atop the six-mile-long edge of a steep dropoff from 90 to 130 feet of water. We would put out an umbrella rig with four tube lures, each tied to 3 feet of light leader, 40 feet behind the boat, attach it to the clip on the ten-pound lead downrigger ball, and lower the ball to 110 feet. At idle speed, the ball would stream out enough to stay above the bottom, though near it. As soon as a school of pollock appeared on the fishfinder, the boat would be shifted to neutral, and as it slowed, the ball would sink. As the ball struck the bottom, the boat would be shifted into forward, causing the ball to hop up and making the lures on the umbrella describe slow sine waves along the bottom in the exact manner of live sand eels.

The last refinement of our method was in the tube lures themselves. Compared to the ones we used for bluefish, they had to be perfect. Each had to spin freely and wiggle seductively, and the most effective colors were bright reddish-orange and bright green. Years later I ran into a report in a scientific journal on research into fish vision that confirmed that pollock are sight feeders and are particularly sensitive to these two colors at the depth we were fishing.

Skimming the bottom was tricky, and we lost some gear learning the technique, but once all the components were in place it became dependable. We would get on the school, shift to neutral, let the ball drop, shift the boat back in gear, and both rods would go off, each with two to four big pollock. Each pass over the school yielded an average of five or six fish weighing around thirty pounds each. A dozen passes and the wells were full, and we were back to the dock early, everyone happy. Sixty or seventy fish per boat per day, amounting to as much as a ton, was a normal catch. Soon, dozens of charterboats from three states were hammering the jumbo pollock in this one small area. Whatever else was happening in the New England pollock fishery, such slam-bang slaughter was unconscionable and ultimately could not be sustained. Within five years the fishing was over. The pollock disappeared, and they have never returned.

We knew better, and herein lies the "tragedy of the commons." A number of us argued, both on the radio and in groups, for a voluntary limit of thirty fish per boat per day. It would have been easy enough to do, since the customers had no way of knowing where the schools were or when you would go over them. All we would have had to do was slow it down a bit. Thirty fish still would have allowed for a total boat catch of as much as a half-ton, and no group of six anglers has a legitimate need for any more pollock than that. No one dared go first. The argument went like this:

"If I bring in thirty and my competitor brings in seventy, I'll lose my customers." Unfortunately, this argument was flawless, although clearly shortsighted. I have found that such enormous catches are themselves ultimately bad for business. When people grow accustomed to catching a ton of fish they soon become either turned off by the inevitable wastage or turned off when the catches are no longer possible.

• • •

The groundfish, or demersal finfish, that are economically important to New England can be sorted into two groups, which the commercial fishermen call "flat stuff" and "round stuff." The flat stuff is made up of six species of flounders. The round stuff is made up of about a dozen species, the most important of which are in the family *Gadidae,* the soft-finned fishes, which includes the cod, haddock, red and white hakes, whiting, and pollock. The National Marine Fisheries Service (NMFS), in its annual *Status of the Fishery Resources off the Northeastern United States,* lists species as "underexploited," "fully exploited," or "overexploited," depending upon trends in the populations of breeding stocks. By their latest analyses, the only *Gadid* that is underexploited, or capable of sustaining a higher rate of harvest, is red hake, a species that has never found favor in U.S. markets. Cod and haddock are overexploited to a point of devastation where recovery within our lifetimes, particularly for the latter species, may not be possible. White hake, silver hake (whiting), and pollock are listed as fully exploited, or incapable of sustaining greater harvest without depleting the breeding stock.

The trouble with this listing for pollock is that the conclusions supporting it seem firmly held by NMFS, while the data underlying these conclusions are filled with contradictions. NMFS lists the long-term potential catch as 37,000 metric tons (81,400,000 pounds, since 1 metric ton equals 2,200 pounds) per year, on a spawning stock biomass to achieve this long-term potential of 122,000 metric tons (268,400,000 pounds). Yet for two decades the annual catch has averaged 49,600 metric tons (109,120,000 pounds), with only one year (1993) within the target, while the spawning stock biomass has actually risen! At the beginning of the period it stood at 88,000 metric tons (193,600,000 pounds, well below what should have supported the high catch), and at the end it had grown to 142,000 metric tons (312,400,000 pounds). How could this have happened if NMFS data and conclusions are correct?

The short answer, of course, is that the numbers and the conclusions they purport to support are simplifications of what is an enormously complex system. The rise in spawning stock biomass was not even, but included fluctuations of as much as 132 percent. It was at its highest, 204,000 metric tons (448,800,000 pounds) in 1985, at the end of a twelve-year period in which the total catch had actually doubled! Since then, there has been a progressive drop in both catch and spawning stock biomass, although the latter now appears to be rising again.

So what is going on? Obviously there is some other major factor at work that is neither included in NMFS data nor allowed for in its conclusions. Strong year classes appear during times of decline as well as during times of increase. In other words, pollock populations are subject to some sort of natural cycles that have nothing to do with rates of human exploitation and of which we have little understanding. Our goal of "long-term potential catch" does not take this natural fluctuation into account, because our knowledge is insufficient. This lack of complete understanding does not mean that we should give up on management—just the opposite is true! But NMFS should present its conclusions with a bit less certainty, while the rest of us resign ourselves to the need for a more conservative approach to management. I know I don't understand what has happened with the pollock, and I am equally certain that the National Marine Fisheries Service scientists don't truly understand it either.

What are we left with? After all the computer models, hypotheses, and population projections, all I am perfectly sure of is that there are now very few jumbo pollock south of Block Island and the annual spring run of harbor pollock at Point Judith has been gone for years.

CHAPTER 6

Bluefish and How to Ruin a Business

> That bluefish eye stare is corrective of your feelings, though,
> whatever they are, isn't it? It's a contradictory eye. I've always
> been glad I was looking into the eyes of these blues out here
> in the open air. Wouldn't you hate to have that eye glare at
> you under water, in the fish's own element?
> —John Hersey, *Blues,* 1987

I hardly ever book a bluefish charter anymore. It isn't that I don't want to—bluefishing is a lot of fun, particularly with light tackle or with a fly rod. The problem is, hardly anyone ever calls me to go. This is a real change from the seventies, when we would fish for bluefish seven days a week, sometimes two trips per day, for weeks on end. It has nothing to do with the fishery itself. Although the bluefish population has declined over the past few years, the loss of customers occurred earlier.

What happened? We (the charterboat industry) did it to ourselves. The charterboat industry is wholly to blame for the loss of this lucrative and steady business and probably at least partly and maybe largely to blame for the bluefish population declines as well. I have heard it argued that changes in the economy and the structure of our society were responsible for the loss of bluefish business, but this line of reasoning is specious. We had lost most of our bluefish customers before the softening economy of the early nineties began to hurt the so-called working class, and the boom years that followed didn't bring them back. And I say "we" because I was as much responsible as anyone. To see how we did it, let me describe a typical day of bluefishing during the seventies.

The mate, usually a young man, walks down the dock and steps onto the boat at five-thirty in the morning. He opens the deckhouse or cabin, rolls up the curtains, greases the tops of the fishing chair stanchions, and wipes the morning dew from the bridge windows. The captain arrives a few minutes later and opens the bridge, checks engine and transmission fluid levels, starts the engines up, and turns on the electronics. Around six o'clock the customers show up. There are six of them (most charterboats are only authorized to take six passengers, hence are often called "six-packs"). Sometimes they are factory workers or family groups who have set aside a few dollars each week for fishing trips. Other times they are company charters, regular trips arranged by supervisors or salesmen as employee rewards or to entertain customers. (Construction and trucking companies used to be dependable customers, and I remember giving a discount for multiple bookings, one of which was a regular Tuesday trip that lasted several years.) Mates always love the company trips because they often include a long lunch break at Block Island and the tips are reliable.

The mate helps the customers with their coolers and shows them where to stow their stuff, how to use the head, and the location of lifejackets (a lot of boats never bother with this last one, preferring not to start the day with any negative implications). There is some laughter and perhaps a telling of the latest dirty jokes, boxes of doughnuts are opened, coffee is poured from thermos bottles. Then the captain nods to the mate, the lines are cast off, and the boat slips away from the dock.

As the boat idles through the harbor, it is joined by other charterboats, a few lobster boats, and one or two draggers in a procession that moves steadily toward the breakwater. The charterboat captains begin the radio conversations that will go on all day: weather, sports, politics, fishing, the latest scandal, what the mate is doing wrong, what jerks the customers are, and a hundred half-baked opinions couched in clichés and the rhetoric of the uninformed. Passing through the breakwater, the captain brings the boatspeed up to around ten or twelve knots, fast enough for hull efficiency and a comfortable ride, slow enough to save fuel and allow the mate to get everything ready.

The mate brings out four heavy boat rods with carbide guides and sturdy reels that are loaded with three hundred feet of stainless steel wire line and a couple of hundred yards of heavy Dacron backing. Three of them are placed in rod holders along the transom, and one is set aside as a spare. He checks the three-fathom (eighteen-foot) monofilament leaders, usually around 130-pound test, replacing any with nicks or frayed spots. Next, he brings out a dozen or more umbrella rigs. These are wire spreaders with four arms, each of which is tipped with a swivel and a two-foot heavy monofilament leader on the end of which is tied a lure made of a six-inch piece of surgical tube pulled over a 10/0 or 12/0 limerick hook. The limerick-style hook is long and has a double bend, so the lure spins and wobbles as it is pulled through the water. The mate reties any frayed leaders (usually most of them) and replaces torn lures. He then lays the umbrellas along the starboard covering boards (gunwales) or, on some boats, along the deck under the covering boards.

By the time the mate's preparations are complete, the boat is approaching the fishing grounds, usually a reef or underwater structure where bluefish are known to feed. The mate explains the fishing procedure to the customers while the captain slows the boat and turns on his chart recorder to locate fish, although bait slicks and diving, feeding seabirds often put him right on them. As soon as bluefish show on the recorder he nods to the mate, writes down the Loran coordinates, and starts a slow turn to port. The mate picks up a rod, clips an umbrella onto the leader, and starts it out from the starboard corner. Dropping the umbrella with its four lures into the water without a tangle is a bit of a trick, so only the mate does this part. If all the wire is put out without a bluefish hookup, the mate hands the rod to the angler in the port chair, runs out a second umbrella, handing the rod to the angler in the middle, and then a third, handing this rod to the angler in the starboard chair. Usually, though, hookups come before all the gear is out, and the customers quickly find themselves cranking in from one to four bluefish apiece as the boat idles ahead on a slow turn, staying on top of the school.

As the umbrella with its load of fish is reeled to the boat, the mate watches for the three-fathom leader. When it appears at the rod tip, he grabs it and handlines the fish up to the boat as the customer continues to reel, then reaches over, grabs the umbrella at its middle, and swings the whole thing, fish and all, into the boat. He unclips the umbrella, the fish still on, and slides it over to a customer along the port side who removes the fish and tosses them into the fish wells while the mate moves to the starboard side, clips on a fresh umbrella, and starts the rig out again. With the captain keeping the boat turning to port and the mate always letting out fresh umbrellas on the starboard side, on the outside of the turn, tangles with fish being reeled to the boat are avoided. The customer who has taken the fish off the used umbrella then hands it to another customer, who straightens it out and sets it with the others on the starboard side, ready to be used again. The customers rotate positions so everyone gets a chance to reel in fish.

The mate's job is to orchestrate this constant movement of fish coming into the boat and gear going out, and there are a number of tricks that a good mate learns to keep the rotation going while avoiding the nightmare of tangled wire. The result is a factorylike assembly line with fish constantly coming in over the transom on the port side while umbrellas are constantly going out over the transom on the starboard side, and close to a hundred bluefish are in the well before anyone takes a break. By one o'clock the wells are holding over a half-ton of bluefish, and it is time to go home.

On the way in, the mate cleans the reels, repairs any broken wire, and puts the gear away, but he doesn't clean the fish until the boat is tied to the dock. He then empties the wells and brings all the fish up to the cleaning table in boxes or baskets under a sign advertising the boat. This ritual is important to the captain, who hangs around to pass out brochures and cards while the mate fillets the bluefish, which usually number around a hundred and fifty. Knife flashing, a good mate can finish in a little over an hour, while the customers hang around and drink beer, their bonhomie helping the captain's dockside marketing. When the mate finishes with the fish, the captain and customers leave, and he spends another hour cleaning the boat.

That is what a day of bluefishing used to be like. Wire-lining bluefish using this assembly-line method was developed in the sixties when bluefish populations were exploding; it was used by charterboats all along the Atlantic coast. It changed a bit toward the late seventies with the widespread adoption of the downrigger, the device that was so deadly with pollock. The downrigger uses a ten-pound lead ball with a snap release to troll monofilament at depths even greater than were reachable with wire. Because it requires a less skilled mate to deploy than wire and turns can be tighter and made in either direction, most captains were quick to make the change. The end result of the day, however, didn't change.

As deadly as this trolling method was, it paled beside what could be done under the right conditions with eight-ounce diamond jigs. The trolling method worked best on late spring and summer days when the bluefish were spread out and moving about. But at night, or during the day for a few weeks before their autumn migration, they would gather in tight schools to feed. We would find baitfish, anchor on the spot, start chumming, and hold a school of bluefish right under the boat. Each customer would be given a stout boat rod with a fast-retrieve reel (the Penn high-speed 4/0 Senator was generally favored) with sixty-pound test line and a jig with three feet of very heavy leader. The procedure was called "heave-and-haul." The customer would drop the jig to the bottom, put the reel in gear, and reel as fast as he could. If he reached twenty turns he would drop the jig back to the bottom and do it again. In practice, he rarely reached five turns without a bluefish grabbing the jig. The customers loved this method because everyone had a rod in his hands and it was constant action. When a fish was brought to the surface the mate would reach over, take a wrap on the leader, swing the fish in, remove it to a fish well, and toss the jig back in the water; then the customer would drop it straight down for another fish.

The problem, of course, was that the wells filled up too fast. In a couple of hours there would be no place left to put fish, and we would start throwing them back or, if it was okay with the customers, go in early. The fastest I ever saw the well filled was on a late October morning in 1980 on the MAKO II. We had a group of five regulars, four factory workers and a priest, who booked four or five trips every year. They always caught well because they were good anglers, although the four insisted that the priest brought them luck, which was why they brought him. I never begrudged this group a large catch, because at least the fish were never wasted—the priest took them to the parish orphanage. On the MAKO II we were conservation minded by the standards of the day and generally limited our customers to the eleven hundred pounds that would fit in our on-deck fishwell (imagine, eleven hundred pounds of bluefish on rod and reel for *conservation!*). At any rate, the group wanted to see just how fast they could fill the well, so we anchored on a school and threw in some chum. The anglers spread around the rails, each with a boat rod and jig, poised to go, and the priest said a quick prayer; at exactly eight o'clock I gave the word, and they all dropped their jigs. Fifty-two minutes later I tossed the last fish in the well that it could possibly hold.

This kind of slaughter in the name of sport fishing was, of course, unsustainable in the long run—and for a number of reasons other than the obvious one of overfishing the resource. In the first place, people just got tired of it. Initially it is fascinating, and people got caught up in the action and the efficiency possible with "just" a rod and reel (not recognizing the role of precise navigation and fishfinding electronics). But after a couple of trips the thrill was gone as they began to see their role as simply that of a human winch.

Other problems were the quality of the fillets produced at the end of the day and the enormous wastage. The fish were simply thrown into a well, unbled, where they remained for several hours, often in warm weather. By the time they were filleted, the flesh would be turning soft and the blood still in the meat would already be rancid. Many customers told me that they wound up throwing most of it out, and it became generally accepted by an entire generation of anglers that bluefish might be fun to catch but weren't fit to eat. Actually, no fish treated in such a manner is fit to eat, and if it's bled and properly cared for, bluefish is both quite delicious and among the best in nutritional quality. But the damage was done. We had managed to destroy public acceptance of a fish that past generations had regarded highly, and today the suggestion to do some bluefishing is mostly met with upturned noses and references to "sewer trout."

This turning off of an entire customer base began to show up in the early eighties and by later in the decade had put a number of charterboats out of business. Quite simply, the bluefish business died while both the economy and the resource were still strong, and the sole reason was the way the business was practiced. People simply got sick of it.

• • •

The decline in Atlantic coastal bluefish populations in the nineties may have been caused, at least in part, by earlier overfishing. The National Marine Fisheries Service certainly thinks so, though its pronouncements are often suspect. NMFS began gathering data on stock abundance and both recreational and commercial catch in 1974, when bluefish stocks were at a very high point, and while its actual numbers are probably soft, the trend is interesting. During the seventies, the total catch increased steadily to a peak in 1980 of 76,500 metric tons (168,300,000 pounds), of which only 9 percent was commercially caught and sold, mostly by draggers and gillnetters. After 1980 the annual catch steadily dropped, to a low of 18,800 metric tons (41,360,000 pounds) in 1993, a reduction of 75 percent. By 1993, 21 percent was taken commercially, a figure that may be significant in the future.

For bluefish, NMFS considers the long-term potential catch, or the amount that can be harvested year after year without damaging the stocks, to be 30,000 metric tons (66,000,000 pounds) per year. Before 1989, this amount was exceeded in every one of the preceding fifteen years for which there is data, and from 1989 to the present it has not been reached in any year. The reason for the decline, according to NMFS data, is because of a decline in another parameter, known as the spawning stock biomass, or the total mass of breeders. NMFS considers the "spawning stock biomass for long-term potential catch," or the breeding stock required to produce the long-term potential catch plus enough to replace itself, to be 250,000 metric tons (550,000,000 pounds), a number we went below in 1986 and which has continued to decline since. Today, according to NMFS, the spawning stock biomass stands at 81,000 metric tons (178,200,000 pounds), or 32 percent of the total population of bluefish breeders required to maintain a healthy fishery. NMFS now considers bluefish to be "overexploited and at a low level of abundance" and estimates that "fishing mortality rates," or the percentage of the existing population removed by fishing, is now about double the percentage that would allow for a recovery.

Based on these numbers, the Atlantic States Marine Fisheries Commission (ASMFC), the regulatory body empowered to manage inshore fisheries resources along the Atlantic coast, directed NMFS to produce a "Fishery Management Plan for the Atlantic Bluefish," which it did. It was approved in 1990 and went into effect in the member states over the next couple of years. The plan was as much political as scientific, but resulted in most states enacting a ten-fish creel limit for recreational anglers, a number that can be changed from year to year and may at some time include a size limit. It also capped the commercial catch at 20 percent of the total, although, as I noted earlier, it was traditionally less than 10 percent; furthermore, the plan called for no specific controls or quotas until the cap was exceeded. NMFS stated that this provision was to allow for "growth in the commercial sector," a very strange statement after having just declared the stocks to be "overexploited and at a low level of abundance." This transparent dissimulation was immediately protested by recreational fishing groups, who saw it as a gift to politically powerful commercial groups and who feared the long-term implications of any growth in commercial bluefish harvest.

Most fishermen, both commercial and recreational, have accepted the *concept* of management controls because progressive decline of bluefish stocks over the past decade or so is obvious, although not precipitous, and there is the sense that past abusive overfishing is largely to blame. But the specific controls in the Bluefish Fishery Management Plan are widely ridiculed, particularly by recreational fishermen, as both ineffectual and stupid. Ineffectual because, while a ten-fish limit would have been an excellent idea during the slaughter of the seventies, there are now very few days when that limit can even be reached, let alone exceeded. And stupid because few people have much confidence in NMFS population numbers for any fish species. Unfortunately, much of the criticism of NMFS and its data is legitimate.

In truth, the bluefish problem is far more complex than NMFS would have us believe. There is no question that the total catch during the seventies and early eighties was truly enormous. Thirty charterboats from Point Judith sailed three-quarters of their trips from June through early November for bluefish, taking an average of a half-metric ton (eleven hundred pounds) per day, or about 4 million pounds per year. Every night three or four head boats took out large parties and jigged about the same total (many of which were found in dumpsters the next morning). Add to this the fleet of private boats, and consider that Point Judith is but a small port on a long coast with many larger ports, and you begin to see the enormity of the slaughter.

NMFS numbers are static and don't allow for fish movement. In 1984 most of the fishing effort by the entire Point Judith fleet (as well as some Connecticut boats) was directed at an area east of Block Island called the East Ground. A gravelly underwater glacial moraine, it is a superb fishing spot, but covers less than a single square mile! I began to wonder how so many boats could take so many fish from this one spot, day and night, week after week. There obviously was some sort of continuous replenishment, but I couldn't imagine how it could happen so quickly. I finally got a chance to find out one day when my charter, a man with his two children, didn't care to take many fish home. We caught the dozen or so that he wanted and then began to tag and release the rest. One of the other charter captains called to find out what-in-hell I was doing, so I told him and asked how long he thought it would be before my tagged fish were recaptured. He looked around at the fleet and answered, "About twenty minutes." Others chimed in, there was no one who thought the fish would survive more than a few days, and I agreed with them. The actual results were a total surprise. Over the next few weeks I tagged several dozen bluefish, and although a high percentage were recovered, the shortest time any one of these fish was at large was over a month (some survived as long as three years), and *not a single one* was recaptured on the East Ground. Most were recaptured between Nantucket and southern New Jersey, and a few were taken as far as the Chesapeake.

My few dozen tagged fish are not a large enough data base to form many broad conclusions, but a couple of small questions were answered. Schools of bluefish don't settle in on one spot, as we had thought, but move constantly along the coast, back and forth, from place to place. The fish we worked over on the East Ground one day were not the same ones we had worked over the day before or the same ones we would work over the next day. To me, this was a stunning discovery, and I still don't understand why they strike out from a shoal loaded with baitfish to go somewhere else.

This willingness to move about came to mind a couple of seasons ago when I heard two head-boat captains argue that bluefish stocks have not declined nearly as much as NMFS claims. Just in the past few years, they said, they have been seeing huge schools of bluefish way offshore, especially on the outer parts of Nantucket Shoals, outside of the range of day boats. They believe that the major body of bluefish has moved as a result of the decline in sand eels inshore and the explosion of herring offshore, and this body is not properly counted in the NMFS population data. There is, perhaps, a bit of self-interest in this hypothesis, but one of these captains is a friend and a reliable observer, and my limited tagging makes me wonder if there might not be something to it. However, the dearth of juvenile "snapper" bluefish in the estuaries during August over the past several years convinces me that there is a decline, although our response to it is drawn from thin air.

The cause of the current decline remains unproven. This statement seems absurd in light of the wasteful slaughter of the seventies and the data from NMFS. But the data is thin, some of its interpretation is faulty and circular, and it involves too many "round" numbers with little or no support, such as the NMFS figure of 250,000 metric tons for the spawning stock biomass for long-term potential catch. Of course, we need population data as reference points for management and allocation decisions, and it is one of the jobs of NMFS to gather it. But fish don't live inside computers, and their numbers aren't bank accounts that can be easily manipulated in predictable ways. For long periods in the past, bluefish have disappeared along the coast for reasons we can only guess. And there are a lot of fishermen today who believe that we may be entering one of those periods.

In their landmark work, *Fishes of the Gulf of Maine*, Henry Bigelow and William Schroeder chronicle bluefish population fluctuations from the earliest colonial times, describing "brief terms of years" when "they have been known to swarm . . . for several summers in succession, they may then be so rare over periods of many years that the capture of a single fish causes remark."

Bluefish were common during the early colonial period, although no precise records were kept. In 1764, however, they disappeared, at least throughout New England, and were very rare for the remainder of the eighteenth century. They reappeared south of Cape Cod around 1810 and north of the cape in 1837. By 1850 they were swarming all along the coast and were reported to be doing much damage to the mackerel fishery. By the 1880s they had disappeared again, and then they made a moderate reappearance in the 1890s, which culminated in a banner year in 1901, when one school in Narragansett Bay was reported to be over five miles long. A sudden decline lasted until the 1920s, when they again became abundant. In the early thirties a severe crash made them extremely rare until the late 1950s. A rapid recovery through the early 1960s brought them to the abundance with which we are all familiar and which now seems to be waning.

I remember the first bluefish I ever saw. It was the autumn of 1957, and I was one of perhaps a half-dozen anglers casting plugs for striped bass from a place we called Elephant Rock. Suddenly, about a hundred feet out, the water erupted with swirling fish. Everyone cast into the melee and hooked up almost immediately. The fish were only about three pounds each and came in easily on our big surf rods. I had no idea what they were; nor did anyone else except for one old graybeard who looked down at the fish flopping on the rocks and said, "Them's bluefish. I ain't seen one in years!" Over the next few years I saw many more and came to know them well.

NMFS statisticians may not have it completely right, but Bigelow and Schroeder made another observation that should give pause to anyone who thinks the current decline is entirely the result of a natural down cycle. "We ought perhaps to add that it is only in the northern part of its range that the American bluefish falls periodically to a very low level." The current decline is happening along the entire coast.

• • •

Whatever the future holds for the bluefish, whether it be recovery to abundance or another quarter-century disappearance, it is clear that we can never again abuse the species as we did. If this sounds like a *mea culpa,* I suppose that it is. For those rare occasions when I can actually convince someone that bluefish are worth booking a charter for, I have evolved a far different method of fishing. Now we most often use light casting, spinning, or fly rods, but even when we troll, the assembly line method is out. When the fish is brought aboard, I immediately bleed it and then quickly fillet it and put the fillets on ice. As a result, we sometimes spend some time off the fish, but to my amazement we still catch as many fish as everyone wants.

The real difference is revealed in the quality of the meat. The fillets are light and firm with no dark spots from rancid blood. And, surprise of surprises, whether they are smoked, grilled, Cajun blackened or cut into pieces, rolled in batter, and deep fried, they really are delicious. Bigelow and Schroeder call bluefish "an excellent table fish." The early colonial settlers considered them to be "better meat than the salmon." All that is required, as with any meat, is that it be properly handled and cared for.

Another difference is found in the quality of the sport. People go fishing for entertainment, camaraderie, relaxation—in a word, recreation. Our assembly-line method racked up big numbers, but most of our customers were trying to *escape* a rat race, not enter a different one. On suitable tackle, bluefish fight hard and are a *lot* of fun to catch, as some people, myself included, are rediscovering.

Now I only hope that our penance to the fishing gods for our prior sin of gluttony is neither long nor severe.

CHAPTER 7

Sharks; Perceptions and the Importance of Good Science

This time the fish attacked from below. It hurtled up under the woman, jaws agape. The great conical head struck her like a locomotive, knocking her up out of the water. The jaws snapped shut around her torso, crushing bones and flesh and organs into a jelly. The fish, with the woman's body in its mouth, smashed down on the water with a thunderous splash, spewing foam and blood and phosphorescence in a gaudy shower.
—Peter Benchley, *Jaws*, 1974

During the time when the *Jaws* movies were getting wide attention, I received a very strange phone call. It started out normally enough. The caller, a woman, asked a few questions about chartering a boat and, getting more specific, about sharks. When I began to explain our technique for chumming them up and getting them to take a baited hook and what each person in the group would do, she said, "Oh, no, there's not a group, there's just me, and I don't want to use a fishing rod. I have an M-14, and I want you to chum them up so I can shoot them."

I was stunned. My first thought was that she was joking,

but there was a sort of tightness in her voice, and my next thought was that she was deranged.

"Why would you want to do that?" I asked.

"Because I *hate* them," she answered.

"Have you ever been out on the ocean?" I asked.

"No."

"Have you ever seen a shark?"

"No, but I *hate* them. I hate everything *about* them."

I told her she didn't need a charterboat, she needed a psychiatrist, and hung up.

The initial effect of Peter Benchley's book and the first *Jaws* movie was to rouse a deep and primal human fear. It is the terror that lives under the predator's gaze, programmed into our psyche, and our mastery of the planet has not eliminated it. It is the fear of our childhood nightmares, of the dark; it is our horror at being simply eaten, finding the sum of our lives and our total value accounting for nothing more than a quick meal for an indifferent and unemotional predator. Benchley didn't intend to portray the shark as man's ultimate enemy, nor did he foresee the sometimes ludicrous, sometimes tragic results of his work. To his distinct credit, in recent years he has renounced the foolishness and become an articulate spokesman for marine conservation and for an understanding of the proper role of sharks in the marine ecosystem.

Benchley's self-recrimination seems to me a bit misplaced, though. For one, *Jaws* is actually a good book (and I loved the first movie, although the sequels were tiresome and boring ripoffs of the original idea) as long as the great white shark is seen as metaphor, like the great white whale in *Moby Dick* or the malignant robot in the movie *Terminator.* For all the initial foolishness, in the long run the *Jaws* phenomenon had a positive effect. After the hysteria died down, an enormous number of people (I have never since met anyone who claims to have neither read the book nor seen the movie) had been infused with a new awareness of the ocean and respect for its ancient creatures. Books and television specials proliferated, and their popularity made it easier to find funds for legitimate research and for marine conservation. We had whistled past the darkened graveyard and, in the sunlight of knowledge, could all laugh at our silly fears.

It seemed no one was immune from the *Jaws* phenomenon. The woman caller with the rifle was perhaps a most extreme example, but only by degree. There were also the "macho boys," playing out their own little heroic fantasies in expensive shark games. The marina where I kept my boat in those days had a few of these types, and one of them had a slip directly across the dock from mine. He had named his boat LA PESCA MATANCERA, which, he explained, meant "the monster fish," although I am not sure just which language he was using. He said he had chosen the name because he and his crew were shark hunters, and the name was painted across the transom in bold, black script. The boat was about twenty-eight feet long, made of lightweight fiberglass, and built to a design that looked more like a flying saucer than anything that would long survive hard use on the ocean. He and his pals, all city boys, swaggered around the dock a lot, drinking beer and posing, big-game fishing rods with huge Penn Senator reels always conspicuous in the boat's rod holders. One evening after they came in from a trip (I still don't know if they ever caught anything) one of them was sitting, shirtless, in the fighting chair, rubbing down a rifle with a rag as if it had seen use. In the spirit of friendliness, I asked, "What caliber is that gun?"

"Oh," he responded, "this is a thirty-ought-six."

I just shook my head in acknowledgment and turned away in mild disgust. I recognized the rifle as a Marlin Model 336, a light and handy lever-action carbine that has never been made in 30-06 because the design is not strong enough for such a powerful cartridge. And even this jerk's *voice* had a swagger.

That was a quarter-century ago, and back then most everyone who fished offshore carried guns on their boats, supposedly to dispatch any unusually large or aggressive sharks that might get out of hand, although some people routinely shot any shark when they got it near the boat. When I started shark fishing I carried a .357 Magnum in a locker down below, but I didn't keep it for long. A handgun is intricate and in a marine environment requires frequent disassembly and oiling. The newer stainless steel models hold up better, but the springs aren't stainless and sit, hidden, silently rusting. I knew a marine conservation officer (what we call a "clam cop") who carried a stainless revolver in his work on a state enforcement boat. One day on the range he cocked it and pulled the trigger, and nothing happened. When he took the gun apart, he found the mainspring had broken where it had rusted nearly through, and he breathed a sigh of relief that it hadn't happened at a more inopportune time. I found I only used my .357 to take an occasional potshot at a floating can or bottle, and I soon realized that the last thing I wanted to do after ten or more hours offshore was sit down and clean a gun, so the revolver was retired after a single season.

But I was still concerned about the possibility of an encounter with an unusually large and aggressive shark, so I replaced the revolver with an inexpensive, although reliable, single-shot 12-gauge shotgun. With a couple of boxes of slugs and buckshot I figured I could handle most anything, and that gun did turn out to be more practical to keep on the boat. Disassembly and cleaning was much simpler than with the revolver and, by storing it in a case with an oily rag, was only required about twice a month. But in three years I never once even uncased the gun except to clean it. By then I had developed my big-game fishhandling skills to a point where the gun was of no use, so I began to neglect it. One day I opened the case and found deep rust pits in the barrel, so I took the gun home and have not carried one on the boat since.

I had come to the conclusion that, for the most part, guns on a boat are a simply a pain. In addition to the problem of maintenance, there is the obvious danger of an adrenalized and possibly unskilled person running around on deck with a loaded gun, and there is the danger to other boats from a ricochet off the surface of the water. Once a boat about two hundred yards from me fired three times at a shark, and we heard the whine of one bullet passing over our heads. Even Ernest Hemingway once shot himself through the legs while trying to shoot a shark in the water.

With sufficient experience, most big-game anglers finally come to the conclusion that shooting sharks is both stupid and unnecessary. I am not against killing a shark (or any other fish) if it is to be eaten, but simply shooting one for no purpose is psychopathic. Furthermore, sharks intended for food are best killed by some other method than gunfire because a shark must be bled out to produce high-quality meat. Sharks osmoregulate by maintaining a high level of urea in their blood that, if not removed, taints the meat with a distinct odor of ammonia. The blood is best removed while the heart is still beating, which is much less likely with a bullet through the brain. Actually, any shark can be handled by a competent crewmember without firearms. The International Game Fish Association (IGFA) considers shooting fish to be unsportsmanlike and disallows any fish that has been shot from entry in sanctioned tournaments or for world-record consideration.

My objection to guns on boats, therefore, is practical, not anti-gun. I am an avid hunter and target shooter, I enjoy skeet and sporting clays, and I am opposed to restrictions on responsible private ownership of firearms. I just decided long ago that there isn't a whole lot of *use* for most guns on boats, at least there isn't for big-game fishing, including shark fishing.

There are circumstances in which it is appropriate to carry guns aboard. Many years ago I took a boat from Florida to fish the Bahamas, and upon the recommendation of the Bahamian government, we carried a .44 Magnum and two semi-automatic assault-type rifles with large-capacity magazines and plenty of ammunition. It was suggested that we take other precautions as well to prevent our boat from being hijacked by drug runners and ourselves from being killed (witness eradication). I was leery of taking this type of armament into a foreign port, but Bahamian customs checked the guns in as normal equipment without comment. We fished for a week in remote waters, and although our time passed without incident, the very real potential for trouble made me glad that we were so heavily armed.

An increasing number of violent incidents on the water in recent years has me now reconsidering the wisdom of remaining unarmed. Although we have had no problems with drug hijackings in the waters I fish, I have recently seen four newspaper reports of armed robberies committed by people in small, fast boats who approached their victims pretending to need directions or some other type of assistance. A couple of years ago I saw a man shoot from his flying bridge into the water in front of another boat that had cut him off as he was approaching a school of tuna, and a local charterboat had a load of buckshot fired through its unoccupied tuna tower under similar circumstances. The year after that I was tuna fishing with a charter from Boston, a doctor with his father and two sons, when an incident occurred between two other boats near us that ended in gunfire. Afterwards, the doctor, whose conversation had led me to pick as politically liberal, said to me, "I assume this boat is properly armed."

"No," I replied, "I don't carry any guns aboard."

"I'm surprised," he responded. "We're a long way out from any help, and I think it is irresponsible to be unarmed."

Intrigued, I asked, "What would you consider properly armed?"

"An interesting question," he replied, "since I hate guns and have loudly opposed anyone owning an assault rifle. But on this boat, with the lives of customers in your hands, an assault rifle would seem to be appropriate."

I was stunned. This man was intellectually gifted and urbane and had probably never fired a gun in his life, yet concluded that my boat should be armed—and with an assault rifle no less. I thought about his words at length and for the first time began to feel just a little bit uncomfortable at being sixty or more miles off-shore, away from any help, unarmed. I even went so far as to check the availability of a Ruger Mini-30, a popular stainless-steel semi-automatic rifle that can be equipped with a large-capacity maga-zine. It turned out that there was a long waiting list, so as yet I have not placed the order, nor have I really decided to.

• • •

Another effect of the *Jaws* phenomenon was the use of fishing tackle far heavier than is needed for most of the ocean's sharks. Big 10/0 or 12/0 reels with line that tested at 130 or more pounds were pretty much standard in those days, and a 9/0 reel with 80-pound test line was considered on the light side. Such tackle would perhaps be appropriate for the largest of the white, mako, tiger, and thresher sharks, but such fish are uncommon. Most sharks of the coastal North Atlantic weigh less than 150 pounds and, with the exception of the mako, are not very power-ful fish. Their metabolic rates and swimming speeds tend to be slow and except when actively feeding, they are not particularly aggressive (the mako, once again, being an exception). On light tackle they are often spirited, but when overmatched by too heavy tackle they offer no more than a little desultory resistance. Most of the macho shark hunters of the *Jaws* era became bored (short attention spans and a shallow outlook also had a lot to do with it) and moved on. A few of them grew up, started using lighter, more sporting tackle, joined the shark tagging program, and wound up contributing to our knowledge of shark populations and migrations while having some real fun.

As the *Jaws* furor died down, the pendulum swung the other way. Fishermen who had been using too-heavy tackle began to think of sharks as closet wimps with an overblown reputation for ferocity. The truth, as with so many things, lies somewhere in the middle. The most common oceanic shark, the blue shark (known to commercial fishermen as the "blue dog"), has perhaps the worst reputation among East Coast sharks as a sporting adversary. It's held in low esteem as a result of angler experience with the small females and pre-breeding males that migrate onto the continental shelf in late spring, experience that has led to the now widely held belief that blue sharks are phlegmatic and that stories of them attacking shipwreck victims are pure fantasy. But few anglers fish for blue shark in the autumn, when the large and truly aggressive breeding-age males show up. Using chum and tethered live bluefish, I have been able to produce true feeding frenzies in these sharks—maelstroms of swirling, slashing teeth, growing in size as more zero in, swimming at speeds seldom seen in the blue shark. While it is true that sharks of any species present only a tiny danger to swimmers, having seen such aggressive behavior, I find it no stretch to imagine a frenzy, even of lowly blue sharks, at the scene of a shipwreck, and I surely wouldn't want to be in the middle of it!

The only time I was ever injured by a fish (excepting spine punctures and other minor lacerations), the perpetrator was a blue shark, although the fault was mine. I was fishing a shark tournament with a charter, and late in the day we hooked up a large blue shark that I was quite sure would be at least a placing fish, as long as we got him to the scales within the allotted time. In a hurry, I took the shark too quickly. He was still full of fight ("green" is the term we use) and, while wrestling a tailrope on him, my wrist got slammed between his thrashing tail and the boat's transom. My arm below the elbow went numb, and little pinpricks of blood welled up on my skin from the shark's sandpapery hide. The shark took second place in the tournament, but for two weeks I had to pack ice around my badly sprained wrist every night to reduce the swelling, and I spent the rest of the season with it wrapped in an ace bandage. Whenever anyone asked about the bandage, of course

I said that I had been attacked by a shark. But I guess that was a bit of an exaggeration.

• • •

From the too-heavy shark tackle of twenty-five years ago, the pendulum has now swung about as far the other way as it can get, with some anglers even using fly rods. But for most of my shark trips nowadays I cut the middle, deploying rather light 4/0 tackle while keeping one 9/0 set up and ready to go, in case a truly large mako or thresher shark swims into the chum slick.

The offshore fly-fishing fad was born a few years ago when some of the inshore saltwater fly-fishing hotshots decided to try for really big fish. At first I laughed at the whole idea. It sounded really ridiculous to the practical Yankee side of me, especially since I remembered my boyhood, fishing with my grandfather for Maine trout with whippy little bamboo and fiberglass fly rods and delicate single-action reels. But fly fishing works and sometimes works well, and I now have a fair number of charters each year who catch sharks and even tuna on fly rods, using artificial flies made with materials like feathers and deer hair, both natural and synthetic, tied in patterns to match natural baitfish. A whole new industry has emerged to service this new wrinkle on an old sport, and the new rods, reels, and lines are *not* my grandfather's trout tackle. The rods are made of graphite fibers intricately woven and impregnated with epoxy, the reels are masterpieces of computer-controlled machining, and the lines are coated with various concoctions of the chemist's art. Each manufacturer surrounds its gear with voodoo jargon and an air of secrecy, the stuff is very expensive, and the yuppies love it all.

Before this new fad I had occasionally used flies in saltwater, mainly on small stripers and mackerel, and had even used streamer flies offshore as droppers above a jig on a spinning rod to take dorado. But I probably would have continued to laugh off the whole idea of catching the big stuff on flies if I hadn't actually seen

Harry Templeton do it. Harry's son, Rich, owns the charterboat RESTLESS out of Point Judith, and on days when he isn't booked the two of them often take the boat out and fish together. And so it was, one day, that our two boats were more than forty miles out but less than a hundred yards apart when a good bunch of yellowfin and albacore tuna came through, and Harry decided to throw a fly at them. A moment later Rich called me on the radio, simply saying, "Hey Dave, look over here." Harry was standing in the starboard quarter, his rod almost completely doubled over on itself, hanging on. "I suppose we'll be here 'til tomorrow," Rich said. Harry was whooping like the home team just scored the winning basket in overtime, and every few moments I'd see his hand snap away from the reel like he'd touched a hot stove.

I was busy and couldn't follow the whole thing, so back at the dock that afternoon I walked over to Rich's boat to see how it had come out. Harry was still high. *"I got the fish, I got the fish!"* he cried, laughing and picking up a forty-pound yellowfin tuna by the tail.

"Yeah, but it took him two hours," said Rich, "and look at his hand." Harry had bandages on most of the fingers of his left hand.

Harry ran below and came back up holding a fly rod. "Look what I used," he said, handing it to me. It took a minute, then I exclaimed, "Harry, this is an old Herter!" The reel was an equally old Medalist.

"That's right," Harry said, "an old GBF that I built in the fifties for bass."

"And you took *that* fish with *this?*" I asked. Rich was rolling his eyes and nodding his head.

"That's right," he answered. "Think of what you could do with the really good stuff they make now."

In fact, that was exactly what I was thinking, although the Yankee in me responded, "Yeah, Harry, but they've shot elephants with arrows, which doesn't make it a good idea."

But the idea was there, so the following spring, when I met Ed Hughes, it had been fermenting over the winter. Eddie was an FFF-certified and Orvis-endorsed inshore guide with little off-shore experience, and I was an offshore charter captain with little saltwater fly-fishing experience, so symbiosis seemed indicated. But where to begin?

"Sharks," Eddie said. "Sharks. They're dumber than dogshit, and there are all kinds of records to break."

"Yeah, but how do we get them to take a fly?" I asked. "They hunt by smell. Maybe if we give it some scent?"

Neither of us knew if the International Game Fish Association, which keeps the records, would go along with that, so I called Mike Leach, the IGFA president. He told me that the subject hadn't really come up, so there was no rule against it (it is now, however, against IGFA rules to use any scent on a fly). He also told me that the South Florida guides caught sharks on flies and had found that scent didn't help. I remember thinking that may be true in clear tropical water, but it couldn't hold in our turbid, plankton-filled New England water.

So we put together a couple of twelve-weight fly rods, a five-gallon bucket of frozen ground herring, a flat each of frozen herring and mackerel, a jar of concentrated herring oil, and a couple of commercial fish attractants and headed for the "shark-infested" waters of the thirty-fathom fingers southeast of Block Island. On the way, we stopped to get a few bluefish, down, dirty, and fast, using downriggers and very heavy rods and horsing them in. Chunks of fresh bluefish draw sharks, and I also wanted to try fresh bluefish blood as a fly attractant.

We tried a lot of things that day, mostly based on reasoning and what we knew about sharks. We found out that our reasoning was mostly okay, but what we knew about sharks was mostly wrong. The use of scent is a good example. We set up a chum line with the starboard side into the wind to allow room for a right-handed cast from the transom and then hung the chum bucket off the downwind side. I wanted an early warning when sharks were in the slick, so I took a conventional boat rod, the short stiff type we use for codfishing, and simply tied half a bloody bluefish fillet to the end of the line without a leader or a hook. Then I tied a twelve-ounce sinker above the fillet and let it down to a depth of thirty feet, attached a bright red balloon to float it at that depth, let the whole works ride out about sixty feet from the boat, and set the rod in a rod holder with the reel in free spool and the clicker on. When a shark smelled the line of chum and followed it to the boat, he would, we presumed, grab the fillet, which would pull down the balloon, pull out line, and make the clicker sing. This "strike indicator" may have been a bit of a Rube Goldberg, but it worked like a charm, and today I still use it in exactly the same way.

The problem, though, was with the scent on the fly. We reasoned that a chum fly, a layered white and gray bucktail affair, would be our best bet. Since we knew that sharks hunt by smell, I had been soaking several of the flies in bluefish blood, herring oil, mackerel guts, and even WD-40. A few minutes after we started, the balloon went down and the reel's clicker did an imitation of a Vulcan gun, so I grabbed the rod, locked up the reel, and let the shark cut himself off. Eddie tied on one of the soggy, scented flies and cast it about thirty feet into the chum slick. I watched it sink about five feet and observed a seventy-pound blue shark, slowly swimming toward the boat, pass it by.

"He doesn't want it," I said. The shark was now right next to the boat.

"No claspers," Eddie said.

"Huh?"

"It's not a he, it's a she," he replied.

"Smart ass. You probably screwed it up somehow. Swim the fly up by him, I mean her," I said. But it didn't work. The shark passed the fly, went under the boat, and bumped the chum bucket with her nose.

"Here comes another one!" I yelled. "Put your fly right in front of him!" This one was a male, though smaller. He turned a bit to avoid the fly.

"Maybe they don't like eau de herring," Eddie said.

"Try the bluefish blood," I replied. But nothing worked. I went up in the tower to watch and try to figure it out, but soon the sharks disappeared. We waited as the sun rose to the meridian and the breeze died out. Our drift had almost stopped, and finally Eddie said, "Where'd they go?"

"Maybe they're holding down deep."

"What do you want to do?"

"Let's find out," I said. "Put on a chunk of mackerel and some weight, and let it down."

"That's not really fly fishing. In fact, it's cheating."

"Yeah, but it will let us know if they're still in the slick," I said.

Eddie didn't like it, but he cut off a four-inch chunk of mackerel tail, stuck it on his fly, and attached a twist-on sinker to his leader. Just as he lowered it into the water I snapped a picture from the tower. "Hey, Eddie," I said.

He looked up and saw the camera. "You didn't really take a *picture* of me doing that, did you?" he yelled.

I smirked, "Ha, ha, ha, you'd better be real good, 'cause if I show this around, Orvis will *can* your ass, and your yuppies won't speak to you!" Eddie started to say something, but his rod jerked down, and for the next few minutes he was too busy.

On the way in we dissected the day. I told Eddie that from the tower I could swear the sharks were looking the flies over, rejecting the olfactory input. "Yeah, and those flies didn't *look* like anything but a soggy rag," he replied. We came to the conclusion, a correct one as we later proved, that blue sharks may locate prey by smell and sound, but their final attack is strictly visual. We also realized that we were going to have to bring the sharks closer to the boat and hold them there.

Several days passed before we were both free to go out and try again. This time I didn't bring any scent attractants, but we did stop for the fresh bluefish. I had been thinking about fishing for tuna and how I held them around the boat, and Eddie had been working on making flies to resemble a chunk of bluefish, and now we changed our approach. We set up the drift the same way, but while I rigged the balloon indicator, Eddie chopped a couple of bluefish into two-inch chunks. I tossed a couple of chunks out into the chum slick, and Eddie cast one of his new flies, unscented, into the middle of them to see if they would drift down and away together. We then repeated the process, adding and subtracting weighted sections between the leader and the line until we got it right. When we were ready, Eddie checked his knots and leaders, and I went up in the tower to watch and wait.

Soon the balloon went down, and we had a shark in the slick. Eddie backhanded a few bluefish chunks in front of him and cast the fly. The shark came up, turning his head from side to side, looking. One of the chunks disappeared into his mouth and then another; then, still turning, he saw the fly, and it disappeared too. Eddie pulled the line with his left hand and swept the rod back to set the hook, and the fly came whistling past his ear.

"I'll be goddamned," I said.

"What the *hell!*" Eddie said. "He *picked* it *up!*"

From the deck, Eddie hadn't seen what happened. "Eddie, he *saw* the fly, then he *sucked* it in and *blew* it out, slurp-whoosh, just *exactly* like a brook trout with a nymph fly!" I had crazy mental images of brook trout in my shark slick and of sharks lying in a pool in a mountain stream. "He *tasted* it, Eddie; he *tasted* it, and when it wasn't real, he blew it out, just as quick as a trout. This is gonna be just like nymphing!" The oft-heard hypothesis that white sharks bite humans but then spit them out without eating them began to make sense.

By then there were three more sharks in the slick, and by the end of the day we had seen perhaps thirty. We found that we could hold them within visual range by keeping a few chunks of bluefish in the water. They seemed to get used to eating the two-inch pieces and readily picked up the similar-sized fly. But the hookset had to be instant. If the hookset was a bit late, the fly would often lodge in the shark's pectoral fin, the result of constant head turning as it looked for more chunks. We also found that a straight-up hookset was best, sinking the hook in the upper jaw and keeping the leader away from the more set back lower teeth.

Once we had worked out these problems, we began to hook up a lot of sharks, sometimes three dozen or more per day. But my old methods of fighting big fish on conventional gear didn't work very well with fly rods, and in the beginning we lost most of our sharks to broken leaders. One day, while we were still very low on the learning curve, we made an arrogant attempt to set a world record in the new twenty-pound leader tippet class. We had been playing with small sharks, using a three-foot steel shock tippet at the end of the leader, when a large shadow ghosted up from deep in the slick. It was a male blue shark of around two hundred pounds. Eddie reeled in and switched to a fourteen-weight rod with a regulation IGFA leader while I scattered bluefish chunks. He had to yank the fly away from a couple of smaller sharks before the big one finally, lazily, inhaled it. Eddie set the hook, but the big fish showed no response and actually continued to feed. He swam under the boat, and Eddie squawked and dropped his rod tip as far into the water as he could get it and yelled, "He doesn't know he's *hooked!*" The fish turned toward the stern and, as the line appeared from under the transom, shook his head and took off, down and away.

"He just figured it out," I said.

Eddie held the rod in close, tip up, and let the big fish run against the bend of the rod and the drag. I started the engine and came back to the after control station, my usual position for fighting a big fish with the boat. At half-spool I backed down to slow the loss of line, and when the fish stopped I spun the boat to starboard to recover line going forward. But even at idle speed the fly reel couldn't keep up. Eddie reeled like a madman, but the line went slack, and I had to drop out of gear. Fortunately, the fish stayed on, although Eddie and I heaped verbal abuse on one another.

I compounded the verbal abuse when the shark made a sudden hard run and Eddie "bowed" to the fish and stripped out line with his left hand, a tarpon fishing maneuver. The shark rolled over the leader, broke it, and was gone. I explained to Eddie with great emphasis that he should never, never, do that again. Later, I ate crow when we started getting makos on a fly. Makos jump, sometimes twenty feet into the air, and we discovered that "bowing" the rod tip below horizontal and pulling off a quick bit of slack is *exactly* the correct maneuver to keep them from landing on a tight leader and breaking it.

As we climbed the learning curve, sharks became to our big-game fly fishing as green-circle slopes are to skiing—a great place to start and an equally great place to tune up rusty skills at the beginning of a new season. But above this basic level, there is a higher plane, attainable by the expert angler. Charlie Valentine, who manufactures the Valentine line of fly reels, was the first angler on my boat who could detect a pick-up and set the hook on a shark by feel alone. Several times he hooked up before the shark could be seen in the slick. He was with his son and two other anglers, and I became so confident in this group that later, when we had a dozen sharks in the slick and two rods on, and then three, I said, "Put out the fourth rod!"

Eddie said, "Four on at a time? *No way!* We'll wrap them up and lose *all* our gear!"

I replied, "Remember, Eddie, *de l'audace, encore de l'audace, toujours de l'audace.*"

Eddie looked at me, shook his head, and said. "Asshole, *encore* asshole, *toujours* asshole."

But Charlie and his group were magnificent, dancing

around one another, bringing the sharks up one at a time, and Eddie never missed with the stick as he tagged and released every one.

• • •

The Cooperative Shark Tagging Program began at the Sandy Hook Marine Laboratory of the old Bureau of Sport Fisheries and Wildlife (now the U.S. Fish and Wildlife Service in the Department of Interior) at Sandy Hook, New Jersey. The first director of the lab, Dr. Lionel Walford, had started doing research on sharks with a longline survey in 1961. The following year one of his young scientists, Dr. John Casey (Jack to his many friends), began testing tags and tagging procedures. In 1963 the formal tagging program was established as an offshoot of the original research, with Jack Casey directing seventy-four volunteer taggers from the commercial, charter, and sport-fishing fleets.

The program grew at a steady rate, with 561 sharks tagged in the first two years and 3,400 in the first five. A government reorganization brought the program into the National Marine Fisheries Service of the Department of Commerce, where it became part of the Apex Predator Investigation with Jack Casey as its director, and in 1966 it was moved to its present location at the Northeast Fisheries Science Center in Narragansett, Rhode Island. By 1971 close to 10,000 sharks from thirty species had been tagged, and there had been 297 returns from eleven species. In 1978, foreign vessels fishing in American waters joined, and by the mid-1980s around 6,000 sharks were being tagged every year. As the new century began, the Cooperative Shark Tagging Program had over 6,000 participants in several countries, all of whom are volunteers (just *think* about that!). Since the inception of the program, participants have tagged and released more than 150,000 sharks, and 4.5 percent of them have been recaptured by anglers and commercial fishermen from fifty countries. The returned tags have given us our first knowledge of shark population levels, migrations, and social structures.

Over the years, Jack assembled a small but talented group of field biologists and graduate students, and the program expanded into shark breeding biology and physiology. It also became a testing ground for new technologies employed in electronic and satellite tracking; monitoring shark locations, movements, and physiological states; and recording the water temperatures and depths through which sharks travel. The program has had an enormous scientific output, and when I spoke with Jack recently he said, with evident satisfaction, "We now actually know something about the natural history, breeding biology, and migrations of several species of sharks, and unlike the swordfish and other apex predators, we were able to do it before they were decimated. Now they can teach us far more, not just about themselves, but about the other species with which they interact and about the biological and physical structure of the ocean itself."

Unfortunately, "before they were decimated" may have been prophetic. Recent data has shown declines, some very serious, in most shark populations. Sharks, as we now know, are slow growing and long lived, with rather low reproductive rates, which makes them very susceptible to overharvesting. Recent economic expansion in Asia has produced an enormous market for shark products, especially dried fins, which are used in shark fin soup. The result has been the establishment of an unregulated and apparently unsustainable shark fishery, followed by rapid population declines. The National Marine Fisheries Service responded to this threat in their usual manner of "too little, too late, and too slow" by drafting a proposal for a "Fishery Management Plan for Atlantic Sharks" in 1989, which then went through three years of review, hearings, and revision. The final regulations went into effect in 1993, setting quotas and bag limits that are generally regarded as totally insufficient. They also prohibited the unsavory practice known as "finning," or cutting the fins off a live shark to be dried, sold (for up to thirty dollars per pound), and exported in bulk for shark fin soup, although there is no discernible enforcement of this prohibition.

On the other hand, the Cooperative Shark Tagging Program has been an enormous success, for two reasons. One is Jack Casey himself, who directed the program for thirty-two years, until his retirement in 1995. Jack is a burly, straight-talking man, with a tanned, slightly weather-beaten face that still manages to look very young for its years. He reminds me of Steinbeck's character Doc in *Cannery Row* and *Sweet Thursday,* a rigorous and precise scientist who has not forgotten that science is also great fun. He is at home not just in the laboratory, but also at sea, on the docks, or drinking beer with a bunch of fishermen. He is enthusiastic without being overbearing and has the gift of teaching without being didactic and listening without belittling. George Reiger once described Jack as a "national treasure," and I doubt that any of the thousands of people who know him—scientists, anglers, charterboat captains, commercial fishermen, marina owners, fish buyers, deck hands, and even a few politicians—would disagree.

The other reason for the program's success is less tangible. The whole idea caught the imagination of a great many people who were willing to join in. There is something soul-satisfying about luring and capturing an ancient and mysterious animal, a predator at the top of his food chain, tagging him, then releasing him to wander unknown realms, not knowing when, if, or where, he may again be seen. We have become the stewards of the oceans and as such must keep a watch over our responsibility. Wes Pratt, one of Jack's team, has called sharks "the perfect environmental benchmark to the health of the oceans." And I know that a world without sharks would be a world whose soul had been sadly diminished.

CHAPTER 8

Bluefin; The ONE AND ONLY, Part I;
Twilight of the Giants; The ONE AND ONLY, Part II

Each year, at the approach of summer every man who has
fished for flounders and weakfish in the bays and for other
bottom-feeding varieties in the ocean feels the desire to go
farther offshore and try his hand at catching one of the
greatest fighters of all the oceans of the world, the
blue-fin tuna.
—S. Kip Farrington, Jr., *Fishing the Atlantic,
Offshore and On,* 1949

In between fishing expeditions, big-game fishermen go
around lifting Percheron horses off the ground and pulling
loaded freight cars with their teeth. In the evening, they
gather in small groups and feel each other's muscle.
—Ed Zern, *To Hell With Fishing,* 1945

Giant tuna is the term used for bluefin tuna about nine or
more years old and weighing three hundred or more
pounds, and giants are to saltwater anglers as the Himalayas are to mountain climbers. Some may claim indifference to
them, and the majority of fishing's legions will never catch one,
but for most anglers who cast a hook into the ocean there is a sense

that their list of life's experiences is incomplete until they pit their skill and stamina against one of these behemoths. Even the mightiest marlin seems slightly effete by comparison.

Why does the giant tuna stand in such regard? Because, in addition to his potential for great size—the current world record is a tad under fifteen hundred pounds—the bluefin tuna is, pound for pound, the strongest fish that swims.

The bluefin uses raw power to produce his other defining characteristic, speed. The bluefin tuna is at the apex of his food chain, a predator of the open ocean, and he chases down his prey and engulfs it in a burst of amazing speed. His whole body is adapted to moving through water at high speed, from his pointed nose through his teardrop shape, his hard and smooth outer skin, the slots and grooves that enclose his fins at high speed, his drag-reducing finlets, to the hard crescent of his driving, scimitar tail. Even his immense adult size contributes to the goal of outswimming every other ocean creature.

But speed through water is expensive, as any boatowner can attest. I can run the EARLY BIRD at twelve knots on about five gallons of fuel per hour, but sixteen knots consumes about eight gallons. In other words, for a third more speed I need far more power and must invest sixty percent more energy in the form of fuel. To double my speed to twenty-four knots would not only require a much bigger engine to generate still more power, but would also require four times the fuel I burn at twelve knots. Exactly the same physical laws and limitations apply to bluefin tuna, yet giants can swim in bursts over fifty knots. How do they produce enough power for such speeds?

Just as the bluefin's external anatomy is adapted to produce blazing speed through water, his internal anatomy is equally adapted to produce the driving power required to attain that speed. He has a huge engine—three-quarters of the bluefin's body weight is muscle. Even his internal organ cavity is reduced in size to make room for muscle, although this adaptation requires that he spend most of his time hunting and eating. All this muscle is supplied with fuel, and the oxygen to burn it, by a turbocharged cardiovascular system driven by a large and powerful heart. Hemoglobin-rich blood courses through huge gills, pulling oxygen out of the water and sending it to the muscle cells along with a cargo of energy-rich food molecules. Once in the cells, the efficiency of the energy-yielding metabolic reactions is increased severalfold by raising their temperature several degrees above that of the surrounding water—the bluefin tuna is a warm-blooded fish! There are a few other warm-blooded fish, including the other true tunas and the fast-swimming mako shark, but none has the feature so well developed. The bluefin tuna, above all other species, tweaks the last bit of power and speed that it is possible to get out of a fish body.

· · ·

Danny Maclean never rigged his tuna baits until he was under way. It had taken him too many years to learn the little tricks that made them work to give it all away to prying eyes on the dock. He was also careful to have everything put away before he got back in after a trip—except that sometimes he would leave something out so that people wouldn't think he was unfriendly and stop telling him things that might prove useful. But what he left out was always stuff that didn't work. Even when Rick started to meet the boat in the afternoon he continued the charades. The boy loved boats but had never shown much interest in fishing, so the deceptions didn't seem important.

Until now, that is. Eighteen years old, strong, and proud of his strength, Rick had told his dad that he wanted to tackle a giant tuna in the fighting chair. Caught by surprise, Danny had stalled. "It's not a cakewalk, you know," he said. Danny wanted it very badly, but it had to be right.

"You don't think I can handle it?" Under his shirt Rick was flexing his arms and the muscles of his chest and shoulders.

"No, it's not that," Danny had replied. "You'll handle the fighting chair all right. But it can be a long damned time before you raise a fish. Linton used to say it was hours of boredom and moments of sheer panic. Sometimes it goes on for days." In the end, of course, it had been agreed upon. There had been some fish seen at twenty-four fathoms, and Danny had a three-day stretch with no charters booked.

They left in the dark, the heavy boat even heavier with extra fuel. They had plenty of supplies and a hundred pounds of mackerel in brine plus another hundred on ice, and they would stay out "until we kill a big fish," Rick had told his stepmother. Danny thought to himself that they would probably run to the lee of Block Island to anchor up at night, particularly if it got rough or the kid got seasick. Clear of the harbor, he shut off his running lights and changed course, set the autopilot, and settled in to a comfortable, steady fourteen knots. Rick went below and curled up under a blanket in the port berth, but Danny knew he wouldn't sleep.

An hour later it was getting light, and Danny went below and shook his son's shoulder. "Time to get to work," he said. Rick pretended to be waking. He rubbed his eyes, but sprang right up. Back on deck, Danny saw bright anticipation in his son's eyes. A flush of envy for the boy's undamaged wonder passed through him and was gone, replaced by guilt and determination to not let the bad things happen and hope that they hadn't already.

"The first thing you have to learn is that everything you heard me say at the dock was bullshit, and whatever you saw on the boat at the dock was bullshit," Danny said.

Rick's eyes widened and then he smiled and said, "That explains the course—and the lights."

"What do you mean?"

"You told those guys we were going southwest of the island, but we've been going southeast. And you ran dark."

"It's competitive, Rick. There's a lot of boats, and I do pretty well, and I don't want the jerks all over me."

Danny showed his son how to make a daisy chain of six or seven mackerel in a line with only the last bearing a hook, how to make the piano-wire leader, how to attach the swivel to one end with a haywire twist that wouldn't pull apart, how to sharpen the giant hook to a needle point without weakening it and then attach it to the far end of the leader with a short section that could be quickly replaced "in case a bluefish chops up your hook bait."

"Does that happen much?" Rick asked.

"Lad, you may spend the whole day on your hands and knees sewing mackerel. We call a bluefish attack 'getting slimed'."

He showed him how to debone a mackerel and sew it on the hook so that it would swim properly and the hook would stay put but the thread wouldn't show, how to sew the mouths shut on the other mackerel, teasers without hooks, and attach them in a line up the leader, using a knot that worked like the Chinese fingers puzzle. Finally, he showed him how to attach this elaborately prepared daisy chain to the 180-pound test line from the big 14/0 reels and how to tape the knots so that the probing fingers of moving water wouldn't loosen them through hours of trolling. "Remember one thing," he told his son, "don't ever use the expression 'good enough.' If you even *think* it, you're already wrong. If your rig isn't one hundred percent, then pull it apart, 'cause if you don't, a giant tuna will." He then left the boy to make up five more rigs so that they would have three to troll and three to keep on ice as backups.

Danny returned to the helm, checked his position on the Loran, made a course correction on the autopilot, and listened to radio chatter. He rarely used the radio himself—too many boats had directional antennas—but once in a while a weekender would let slip some useful information. He looked at his son, kneeling on the deck sewing mackerel, then looked at the sun, low and bright over the port bow. Good, it'll be calm all day. Maybe he's over it. Maybe we'll even get lucky.

Rick was attaching a teaser mackerel to a leader when he felt the first wave of nausea. He tensed up. Oh no—oh shit! He lifted his face into the breeze, stared at the horizon, went back to sewing. He detested seasickness or, more precisely, the fact that he got seasick. As a child it had made him feel weak, unworthy of his family's seafaring tradition. He would hate himself when it happened, hate the loss of control, hate the boat, hate the ocean, hate the fish. Most of all he would hate his father, the one man in the world he wanted to impress.

Danny went below to get the safety lines and the harness. When he came back on deck Rick was hanging over the side, retching deeply.

"All I see is an asshole and two elbows."

"Reeeetch!"

"How's the bottom paint look?"

Rick knew the routine. The next line would concern "praying to the sea god Ralph." He remembered his father putting that one on the radio ten years before on the second worst day of his life. The very worst day came a year later when his mother got the court order that kept them apart for six years. He stood up and turned.

"Bottom paint's fine. So are your fucking zincs."

"Wash your face. You look like hell. Gonna make it?"

"I'll make it if I have to carry a goddamn bucket."

"Well, get a rope and hang it around your neck 'cause you'll need both hands. And don't puke on the baits. It's hard enough to get a tuna to grab one." Danny turned and went back to the helm. Damn, the kid's tough enough, but if it keeps up he'll lose strength. Strength wasn't always important. He had seen a kid who didn't weigh a hundred pounds take a fish over nine hundred. But that kid had experience and he had technique—knew how to pressure the fish, when to relax. Danny knew that with Rick it would be a pulling battle, that he would fight the fish with his arms and shoulders, relentless but inefficient. He would need all his strength for that.

A half-hour later they were in deep water just off the western edge of what the old-timers called the nineteen-fathom bank but that the new fishing charts called "the claw" from the shape of its contour lines. Danny cut the diesel back to idle speed and reset the autopilot to run east-northeast onto the bank. A quarter-mile ahead he could see the first of the seabirds working the bait schools and ahead of that several boats already trolling.

"Birds," Danny said. "Put that aside, and let's get the gear out. You can finish it afterwards." He climbed up and lowered the outriggers while Rick carefully coiled the unfinished daisy chain in the icebox.

"Okay, I'm gonna show you how to set the baits with tag lines. Jesus, that's a nice shade of green. I wish I could paint my hull that color." Rick's face flushed a little under the waxy paleness. "Let me get my camera. I gotta get a picture, maybe capture it, see if the paint guy can match it."

"Don't take any pictures," Rick said.

"I already did. Got a good one of you power puking. Your ass is in the air, but you can still see who it is. I'm gonna show it to your girlfriend."

"You really *are* an asshole," Rick was shouting now. "I'm going to drop your *fucking* camera right over the side!"

Danny laughed as he let out the first bait. Good, the kid's mad. As long as he stays that way we'll be all right. "Look," he said, "where you set these baits is important. Counting teasers and hook baits you got eighteen mackerel out there, and they gotta look like a panicky school, flippin' and floppin' on top. If any part of it ain't right the tuna'll spook, and you won't get a sniff."

Why does he talk like that on the boat? He's an educated man, but he uses the idioms of a dummy . . . an idiot . . . the idioms of an idiot. Rick almost laughed out loud at the silly alliteration, but he paid attention as his father showed him how to create the predator's illusion and as they rehearsed what each would do in the frenzied seconds after a giant tuna hookup.

By the time all three rigs were out and set to Danny's satisfaction ("Take your time. Set one at a time. Put it out, adjust it, watch it, make sure it's right. One that's working good is better than three that are half-assed!"), they were on the bank. The air was full of seabirds, feeding on baitfish being driven to the surface by unseen predators below. Long-winged shearwaters hugged the water in graceful soaring swoops. Tiny petrels, also known as "tuna birds," hovered like scores of little helicopters just above the water, their dangling feet walking on air, and above all, gulls slowly circled and watched, occasionally diving to snap up a tiny mackerel or sand eel.

While he was studying the skipping daisy chains and watching the birds Rick felt better. Then, kneeling down to finish sewing the spares, the nausea came back. He was sewing and breathing hard when he heard his father yell. "Shit! Slimed!" The starboard outrigger was bouncing, the fish not able to break the rubberband holding the fishing line. Before either of them could move, the port outrigger and then the center rigger started to bounce. "They got 'em all," said Danny.

He looked ahead to make sure they were clear of other boats, and then they reeled in the wreckage of their daisy chains. The first two didn't have a single mackerel that wasn't chopped up or missing, and each had a bluefish on the hook. The third still had three intact mackerel although the hook bait was shredded. Danny quickly bled the two bluefish and tossed them into a fishbox.

"You got one spare finished and one almost done. I'll throw the boat out of gear while you finish that one, and I'll repair this one. That'll get us back into action quick." It will also leave us with no spares, thought Rick. Another bluefish attack would put them out of action for a lot longer. The thought of spending the better part of the next hour sewing up three more spares with his stomach in his throat made him wonder why the hell he had wanted to come out in the first place.

As it turned out, it was a needless worry. They had repaired and reset the rigs and Rick had just begun to make the first spare when a giant tuna struck the starboard rigger bait. Rick, on his knees, heard the slam of the rebounding outrigger, looked up at the rod bent almost to the gunwale, the buzzsaw sound of the reel in his ears as line flew out against the drag, and thought without moving, we must have caught onto another boat. But he heard his father screaming, "Fish on!" and a silent "My god, it's really happening," resounding inside his own head; it was another full second before he could move, but then he was up and running to reel in the others before they could tangle and cost them the fish.

Danny spun the wheel to starboard and ran back to clear away the rest of the gear. "Blind strike," he shouted. "Jesus Christ, I never even saw him come up!" They shoved the port and center rods into forward rod holders, out of the way. "Get in the chair!" Danny yelled as he ran to the starboard rod. More than half the line was already gone as he backed the drag off enough to get the rod out of its holder and, bracing it against his shoulder, carry it to the chair where Rick guided it into the gimbal and locked in the harness snaps to the top of the big reel.

"I gotta back down before I can turn," Danny said as he shifted into reverse, spun the wheel to port, and brought up the engine speed. He disliked backing down hard on a fish. Many boats did it, even to the point of shipping water over the transom, and it sure did look dramatic. But Danny always thought about the one bolt that held the shaft coupling in place and the strain it took in reverse, all of the weight of the boat pulling on it. At high rpm in reverse it could break, and the shaft would pull out. Boats had been sunk that way, and although his rudder would keep that from happening, it would still leave him dead in the water with a lost fish and a big towing bill.

As soon as the outrunning line was over the starboard quarter Danny yelled, "Okay, I'm going hard starboard, get ready to take back line!" He shifted into forward as he spun the wheel to starboard, and as the boat came around, he shoved the throttle forward. Black smoke poured out of the exhaust as the diesel roared, and Danny yelled, "Reel . . . reel . . . reel . . . no slack . . . spin that handle, noooo slaaaack!" And then the fish's first hard run was over, and they had recovered most of the line, and Danny had the boat position right, and he was elated with the pure predatory joy that this pursuit always gave him.

He shifted out of gear and, as the boat drifted, walked back to the chair. Rick was pumping the rod, but Danny saw that for every foot of line he took, the fish, now sulking a hundred yards behind and below, took one back.

"How does he feel?"

"Like a fish."

"No, I mean how big?"

"I don't know, I've never had one before. Not that big."

"Probably between three and four hundred. There's been a few of them brought in lately. A good first fish."

"This isn't so bad. We'll have him pretty quick, Dad."

"Just don't rush it, Rick. It's a small string with a big animal on the end." Danny watched his son gain and lose line as the fish circled, gulping oxygen, preparing for another run. I'm not going to say anything. Let the kid beat himself up a little, at least he hasn't been sick again. He'll figure it out when his arms start to cramp. Good thing this fish isn't a real moose.

When the second run came, Danny raced to the helm. He danced the boat around, backing to port when the fish turned left, spinning to starboard and chasing him when he turned right. He was able to keep the fish off the starboard quarter, where he wanted him, but after another twenty minutes he was beginning to suspect that the fish wasn't as small as they had thought.

"What do you think?" he asked. "Still feel small?"

"He quit running. I'll have him up here pretty quick."

The rod tip started to jump up and down. Rick said, "What the hell?" and yanked up.

"Take it easy!" Danny yelled. "He's just shaking his head to get rid of the hook. You'll *help* him, yanking like that! Remember what I told you, fighting a big fish is like making love to a woman. You need a strong hand but a gentle touch!"

"You fucking male chauvinist pig. I'll bet you never say anything like that to Melissa."

"You bet your ass I don't. I still like to get laid once in a while."

Rick cackled at this, but he eased up when the fish snapped its head.

A half-hour later the fish took off on another of its runs, but this time the line angled upward and to the right.

"He's coming up!" Rick yelled.

"Yes, I think we'll get a look at him," Danny said. But that fish isn't done. The kid's not even turning his head.

The fish broke water a hundred yards astern, pushing a bow wake. Danny saw the broad black head, the yellow finlets quivering, the distance between the dorsal fin and the great black tail, its sweeps hard, strong.

"That fish is no three or four hundred, Rick. He's more than twice that. And he's not beat; he just came up to look us over."

Rick was staring at the fish. His legs were locked against the chair's footrest, his arms down. "He's huge! He's pulling the goddamn boat!"

"If you want this one, Rick, we'd better stop the bullshit

and pay attention." Danny was speaking softly, but with great intensity. "You'll kill this fish with the tip of your rod. Concentrate a hundred and ten percent on that tip. You have to keep it bent all the time! If it starts to straighten up, pull line and get it down! Take a turn, a half-turn, even a quarter-turn. You will beat this fish inches at a time. If I can keep him under the starboard quarter and you keep the tip bent, his head will be turned and he won't get enough oxygen. If he runs, let him go against the drag and drop your arms and rest. But be ready to pull line and keep the tip bent if he turns. If that tip comes up, he straightens his head and gets a gulp of oxygen and the fight goes on longer. Concentrate! Feel his life through that rod tip, and take it away from him!"

The fish sounded and turned toward the boat. The line went slack. Danny dashed for the helm. "Reel! Reel! Reel!" he screamed, but the fish went straight under the boat, trailing the slack line. Still near the surface, he dragged twenty yards of line against the keel before Danny could back the boat away or tell Rick to back off on the drag. When the fish came tight again, the chair spun around but the line and the hook held. The fish sounded while Rick held on.

"That was close, wasn't it?"

"We goddamn near lost him," Danny said.

"Did he know enough to do that?"

"What do you think? A fish that size is no virgin. He's survived twenty years out here. Probably been hooked up and lost before."

Twenty years, Rick thought. He's about the same age I am.

The fish went straight down. "What's he doing now?" Rick asked.

"He'll try to rub the hook out against the bottom," Danny said.

"What can we do?"

"Nothing. Keep the rod tip bent. Concentrate!" Danny kept the boat right over the fish, trying to minimize the angle, the amount of line that could be rubbed against the bottom.

A half-hour later the fish took off on another run. Danny could see the veins standing out on Rick's neck and arms, the sweat on his face. He must be cramping up. He still hasn't learned when to drop his arms, get oxygen. The fish knows more than he does. Got to prove how strong he is. Ha! I was the same damned way. Danny remembered pulling anchors by hand and the arm wrestling matches with other young mates that he wouldn't let himself lose.

"He's running, Rick. You can't stop him. Drop your arms and rest them before they fall off."

"I'm fine! He's the one with a problem." But, Danny noticed, he did drop his arms and shake them.

It was five minutes short of three hours into the fight when the fish came up the second time. This time he was much closer to the boat, and Rick reeled hard, maintaining the pressure as the line arched up. The pointed nose broke water first, and they saw the flash of white as he rolled on his side and sounded. Line peeled off as he went down, but slowly now. "He's beaten," said Danny.

The fish stopped with less than a hundred yards of line out. Rick started to slowly pump the rod again, and this time he was gaining more line than he was losing. Danny set up the deck for killing and securing the enormous fish. He brought out the eight-foot lance with its detachable harpoon point to which was spliced a fifteen-foot length of rope, which he tied to the base of the fighting chair. He then went below and brought up the meathook, also secured to a similar length of rope, which he also tied to the base of the chair, and two tailropes, which he laid on the chair's footrest.

Danny then walked over to the gunwale and said, "Increase the pressure, Rick. He'll hang deep now and circle. You have to lift him. When he circles toward you, take line. When he circles away, drop the rod tip but hold your fingers on the line and don't let him take any back. You'll work him up that way."

Danny stared down into the water, waiting to see the fish. It didn't come. He turned and saw that Rick was still losing line on the turns.

"Increase the *pressure,* Rick! You have to *raise* this fish! Don't *let* him take line!"

"What if he snaps his head again?"

"He doesn't have the strength left. Now put it to him!"

Rick increased the pressure a little, but Danny saw that he still was losing line on the turns. He must be tired. If he would just hold that line. Danny looked back down, following the line with his eyes. He thought he saw a flash of white, stared, then saw it again. Now he could see the fish.

"I can see him, Rick! He's about sixty feet down!"

Rick didn't say anything. He was breathing hard now. Danny picked up the lance, stepped to the right side of the line. He said, "Listen, Rick, we have to do this part right. When you see me strike, if I yell 'It's in,' you back the drag off halfway, set the rod in the righthand holder, jump out of the chair, and pick up the meat hook. Come up on my left side. I'll pull up on the dart line, and as soon as you can, put the point right through his eye. It'll go right into his skull. Then I'll hand you both lines and pick up a tailrope. Once I get him tailroped to a cleat we own him. Want me to go over that again?"

"No. I played soccer five years. I can follow a game plan."

Danny stared at his son for a few seconds, then turned and looked back down into the water. The fish was closer now, making counterclockwise turns, unable to stay upright. But when he turned away he was still taking some line out and getting his nose down. The hook was well set in the corner of his mouth, but Danny could see that on every turn the hole it had

143

made was getting bigger. "He's getting his nose down, Rick. You can't let him get his nose down!" Danny gripped the lance harder, his body tense.

The fish was only twenty feet down when the hook pulled free. The rod snapped up. Rick groaned, his shoulders slumped. Danny watched the enormous fish, still on its side, in tight counterclockwise turns, descend like an airplane in a slow spin into the darkness below.

After about a minute, Rick unclipped the harness, lifted the rod out of the gimbal, and set it into a rod holder. He went to the cooler, took out a jug of ice water, drank some, then lay down on the deck and poured some over his face.

"Want to try for another one?" Danny asked.

Rick opened his eyes and stared into his father's face. "No," he said, "No, I don't." He got up and went below and lay down on the port berth.

Danny stood there for several minutes, watching the sunlight dancing on the ocean. Finally he started putting everything away. Then he set the autopilot on a course for Point Judith and started for home. An hour out he called Melissa on the radio. On all of that long ride back Rick got up only once, to vomit over the side. He was asleep when they passed through the Point Judith breakwater and only woke up as Danny backed the boat into its slip. They washed the boat and cleaned the gear in silence. Walking up the dock to the truck Danny said, "You don't get them all, Rick. In fact, you don't even have any special claim on them until they're tailroped to the boat." Rick didn't say anything.

Later, on the ride home, Rick said, "Will he live?" Danny started to answer, then paused. Finally he said, "I don't know, Rick."

"What do you mean, you don't know?" He turned to the window. "I thought you knew everything."

Danny felt a flush of anger, but he said nothing.

Rick said very little at home and right after supper went to bed. Later, Danny was lying in bed watching the ceiling fan turn when Melissa came in and flopped down next to him. "What happened?" she asked.

"We lost the fish, Mel. It's happened before. It'll happen again."

"No. Something happened to Rick out there. What was it?"

"Nothing happened to him. He's just real disappointed."

She looked at him for several seconds and then said, "He's not you, you know."

• • •

Bluefin tuna are found in warm to cool temperate oceans around the world and have been harvested in nets and fishtraps in the Mediterranean for centuries. More than a century ago they were taken off the coasts of New England and California by harpoon, trap, and trolled or baited handline, although the market for them was small. The first large bluefin taken on rod and reel was a 183-pound fish, caught in 1898 by Charles Frederick Holder off Catalina Island, California. The announcement of Holder's feat electrified the world of angling and is considered to mark the birth of the sport of big-game fishing. Soon articles and books were written, tuna clubs formed, and over the next three decades all the basic methods and equipment used in modern big-game sport fishing were developed.

Holder was criticized in his own time for his unabashed promotion of himself and his adopted state (among other things, he was the originator of the Tournament of Roses parade), and it has been suggested more recently that perhaps his tuna wasn't really the first over a hundred pounds and that if he hadn't done it someone else would have very shortly. Indeed, the argument goes, once the deed was done, as with the running of the four-minute mile or the conquest of Everest, it was quickly repeated by others.

The end of the nineteenth century was a time of new technologies and a zeal for new adventures.

Looking back across a century, one can often feel a sense of inevitability toward the courses taken by events in human history. Although others may have been trying to land a large bluefin with a rod, Charles Frederick Holder was the one who actually did it, told about it, and then promoted it as a new sport. His written accounts of the feat (as well as his other fishing stories) are suffused with a *joie de vivre* that seems more a characteristic of the man himself than simply of his times and, even allowing for the florid Victorian-style writing, are just plain fun to read.

Holder's feat was extraordinary, considering the primitive tackle available to him. His tuna rod was seven feet long and made of split bamboo. His reel had a rudimentary brake to prevent the line from overrunning but no real drag mechanism to pressure the fish other than a piece of leather to force down against the line with the thumb. The line was Irish linen, twenty-one thread, with a break strength under sixty pounds and would quickly rot if it weren't wound on a drum every night to dry. Every morning six hundred feet of line, all that the reel would hold, had to be let out behind the boat to soak, both to increase its strength and to make certain that that first scorching run of a bluefin tuna wouldn't burn through the leather thumb drag and the angler's thumb as well!

Holder's boat was a rowing launch, lightly constructed so the fish could tow it as the boatman frantically rowed after him to help reduce the pressure. The small vessel was occasionally swamped (in waters known to be regularly visited by white sharks), and once when a tuna smashed down upon the gunwale it actually capsized! Without fighting chair, harness, or any other mechanical advantage, Holder fought his first big tuna for close to four hours before it could be gaffed and later confessed "that a few moments more would have placed me *hors de combat.*"

Word of Holder's catch made southern California a mecca for the new sport, and over the next few years scores of bluefin weighing more than a hundred pounds were taken by anglers using a rod, reel, and linen line of no more than twenty-four threads—the fair-catch standard of the newly formed Catalina Tuna Club, including the club record 251-pounder taken by Colonel C. P. Morehouse the year after Holder's first fish.

The sport remained hazardous, injuries were frequent, and truly giant fish unattainable until the development of the heavy reel with a disc clutch drag, a handle that would not turn backwards (many knuckles were bruised and broken by the earlier reels), and a capacity of more than a quarter-mile of thirty-nine-thread line. Along with the new reels came new boats with improved internal-combustion engines and marine transmissions with reverse gears, fighting chairs with gimbals and harnesses, and new knowledge of the ocean's fish and tricks to catch them. By the early years of World War I, southern California's anglers were catching striped marlin and swordfish over four hundred pounds.

But the really big bluefin tuna were in the Atlantic. In 1915 the world record moved to the Atlantic, where it would remain, and after the First World War the attention of the world's big-game anglers shifted there. Tuna clubs were established along the lines of the Catalina Tuna Club, competitions began, and many East Coast charterboats expanded into the new fishery. By the mid-twenties several bluefin over a quarter-ton had been taken with rod and reel from the waters off New England and Nova Scotia, including Zane Grey's 1924 world-record fish of 758 pounds. In 1935 Ernest Hemingway landed the first giant bluefin off Bimini in the Bahamas, and two years later the first international team tuna tournament was held off Wedgeport, Nova Scotia. By then there was a generally accepted code of fair and sportsmanlike angling practice, which was formalized in 1939 with the founding of the International Game Fish Association by Michael Lerner and several other distinguished anglers (Hemingway was one of the original vice presidents) to make and revise tournament angling rules as needed and to keep track of records. The largest bluefin tuna taken to date by rod and reel under the IGFA rules weighed 1,496 pounds and was caught in October 1979 by Ken Fraser off Nova Scotia.

The three decades between the mid-thirties and the mid-sixties are often referred to as the golden age of big-game fishing. While the phrase may encompass some nostalgia, there is much truth in it as well. Comparing then with now, I see two fundamental differences. First, the golden age coincided with the peak of the mechanical age, and electronic devices were primitive or nonexistent. Boats, machinery, and gear were reliable, and no matter how complex, they were understandable and therefore controllable. When he retired, charterboat captain Bob Linton, who had built his own forty-three-foot boat, MAKO II, and whose career spanned the golden age and extended into the years after, told me that the biggest change in his time was a loss of control. "I used to know how things worked," he said, "and if something screwed up I could figure out a way to fix it. These electronics are like magic, but I don't feel like I know how things work anymore." A fisherman in the golden age had to know "how things worked," and it made him feel a part of his boat and somehow closer to the sea and to the fish as well.

The emergence of the electronic age changed this relationship. The alphabet soup of acronym-named devices that are supposed to be no more than tools to make things easier—LORAN, GPS, DGPS, SONAR, EPIRB, VHF, SSB, DSC, RADAR, CANBUS, and so on—have too often become no more than distractions from what we are, or should be, about. Too many sport fishing boats today resemble a video arcade and are operated by people who go fishing but never feel the sea and who would be lost both in spirit and in fact if the electrons ceased to flow through the circuits of their toys. It is not that I cannot accept change—I most certainly would not want to give up my radar when crossing a busy sound in thick fog. But I have witnessed a decline in knowledge of seamanship and navigation and a consequent loss of feeling for the pulse of the sea in inverse proportion to an increase in the use of electronic crutches.

Another reason for the demise of the golden age was the emergence of heavy industrial fishing vessels. Quaint commercial fishing boats in picturesque fishing villages are an anachronism in today's world of factory trawlers, enormous tuna seiners, drift gill-netters, and distant-water longliners, and every offshore fishery in every ocean is under the threat of decimation. Meanwhile, the governments of the world struggle just to figure out how to begin to control the slaughter.

While the golden age may have ended during the sixties, good sport fishing for giant bluefin tuna off New England really lasted through the seventies, although the seeds of destruction had long since been planted. In 1951 the U.S. Fish and Wildlife Service began to explore the possibilities of expanding the Atlantic commercial bluefin tuna fishery and increasing the efficiency of harvest. They concluded that purse seining with large vessels was particularly effective, and four years later the Bureau of Commercial Fisheries (now the National Marine Fisheries Service) offered significant incentives to fishermen willing to try it. In 1958 the F/V SILVER MINK became the first commercial purse seiner to catch Atlantic bluefin tuna. In 1961 a second purse seiner was added, a sardine cannery in Eastport, Maine, was converted to pack tuna, and the fishery took off.

By 1963 there were eighteen purse seiners in the Atlantic bluefin tuna fishery, including several huge vessels from the Pacific, and their total catch that year was 5,770 metric tons, most of which was made up of juvenile fish under five years old and from 50 to 122 centimeters (20 to 48 inches) long. New canneries opened in Maryland and Puerto Rico, and the following year three more vessels entered the fishery. But the catch had already begun to decline and never again reached the 1963 level.

Through the sixties and early seventies the purse seiners continued to target juvenile fish, although several left the fishery as their catches declined due to steady erosion of the stocks. By the mid-seventies it was clear that the population of breeding-size fish (giants) had also begun to decline, apparently due to lower recruitment from the heavily pressured juveniles. Then, in the late seventies, a disaster befell this largely unregulated public resource. Giant bluefin tuna suddenly became the target of a huge and lucrative export market.

The market was Japan, where bluefin tuna, particularly large fish with high fat content, were such a prized commodity that demand almost always exceeded supply. By the mid-seventies, Japan's post-war mercantilist policies had brought both prosperity and an abundance of cash. In a very short time buyers for Japan bid the price of prime giant tuna, which had been worth pennies a pound in the sixties (if you could even find a buyer), to two dollars, then four, ten, twenty, and even thirty or more dollars per pound! A fish that had been hardly worth bringing in suddenly could be sold for many thousands of dollars! A *single fish!* The response, of course, was no different from that of the western gold rushes a century earlier.

By 1976 the purse seiners were shifting their attention from juveniles to giants, and with stunning efficiency they decimated the stocks in just five years. By 1981 the biomass of bluefin tuna in the western North Atlantic Ocean was only 20 percent of what it had been a decade before. To be fair, the purse seiners weren't alone in the slaughter. The gold-rush mentality also infected sport fishermen and multiplied the numbers of harpooners and handliners. But these methods never achieved the deadly efficiency of the purse seine and during the years of maximum slaughter accounted for only a fraction of the catch.

Since the early eighties, bluefin tuna fishing has resembled scavenging on a dying corpse. Efforts to regulate, conserve, and restore the fishery at both the national and international levels have ranged from ineffectual to corrupt. The population continued to decline for another decade, then seemed to stabilize, and now may have actually begun a painfully slow increase, although from numbers so low—only about 10 percent of what we had in 1970—that I do not expect to live long enough to ever again see the enormous rolling schools of giant fish that swim now only in the oceans of my memory.

• • •

Although he hadn't set the alarm, figuring to get a little extra sleep, Danny awoke at his usual four in the morning. He dressed quickly, turned on the coffee in the kitchen, and stepped out onto the back deck to check the weather. It was cool with no breeze and the stars were bright; he breathed deeply, taking in the early summer smells. He stepped back into the kitchen, tapped the glass front of the barometer, and turned on the weather radio. He poured a glass of orange juice, cut a banana onto a bowl of cereal and milk, poured a cup of coffee, and sat down. Danny didn't see himself as a creature of habit, but the morning ritual was so fixed that he would feel a pang of annoyance if, say, they were out of bananas or orange juice.

Finished eating, he poured a second cup of coffee and went downstairs to his workroom. He replaced a broken guide on a boat rod, then took apart a well-used 4/0 reel, replaced a broken pinion gear, reassembled it, and put it in his boat bag next to his logbook, which was the one item he never left on the boat. Then he turned off the lights and went back upstairs. The sun was rising, but he found Mel and Rick still asleep. It was a fine morning to be alone, so Danny headed down to the boat. There had been a time, earlier in his life, when he had been afraid to be alone, although he would not have admitted it then and saw no reason to speak of it with anyone now.

Danny was partway up the tuna tower, threading a new halyard into the starboard outrigger and thinking about lunch when Rick walked down the dock and stopped next to the boat.

"Permission to come aboard, Cap'n?" he asked. He was trying to be flippant, but Danny could see that he was ill at ease.

"Permission granted," Danny replied, "and it is duly noted that you arrived when the work was about done, but just in time for lunch."

"I thought the work was never done. That's what you told me, anyway. I reckon you can find more of it that needs doing."

"Well, since you mention it, the zincs need to be checked, and while you're under the boat you can clean the hull. Also, the downriggers need to be pulled apart and cleaned, and all the boat rods need new line. And there's a hydraulic line with a corroded end fitting that ought to be replaced, especially since I'm chartered flat out after tomorrow, at least 'til Columbus Day. That'll take us up to suppertime."

Rick was looking down the dock, watching a seagull with a green crab, flipping it over, stabbing at its belly with his beak. "Dad," he said, "I was a shit yesterday."

Danny stopped what he was doing and was looking down at him, the end of the halyard in his hands.

Rick turned his head from the gull, looked up and into his father's eyes. "You don't take me very seriously, do you?"

"Yeah . . . yeah, I do, Rick. Trouble is, you take yourself too seriously. You weren't near as hard on me yesterday as you were on yourself. A few years on the ocean and you'll get a feel for just how little you really are."

"I feel pretty little right now. You still off tomorrow?"

"Yeah, you want to go out and suffer some more?"

"I don't know about the suffering part, but I still want a giant tuna." Rick was smiling now, and Danny felt a wave of love for his son.

"Then we sail at five," he said. "Now let's get some lunch!"

The next morning Danny was keyed up, anxious to get started, and by five o'clock they had already passed the outer seawall and were steaming south, straight out to sea. Mel had packed a big lunch for them the night before and had gotten up before they left. She hugged Rick and gave Danny one of the soft kisses that always left him feeling a bit tight in the chest. He figured she and Rick must have had quite a breakfast conversation before the kid came down to the boat with his apology.

Danny set the autopilot on a course slightly west of south and sat back in the helm chair. Rick was standing next to him, watching the sea ahead as it grew brighter with the approaching dawn. "Not going to grab some sleep?" Danny asked.

"Nah, I don't feel like sleeping," Rick replied. "I feel good today. I don't know how to explain it, Dad, but I wasn't ready the other day, and today I'm ready and we're gonna do it."

"Attitude's the biggest part of it, Rick. Nobody wants to hear it, but it's true. You got a negative attitude, you miss the little things that count. Many's the time I've seen someone new outfish the big guns 'cause he didn't know the fishing was lousy or somethin' wasn't supposed to work. They call it beginner's luck, but it's mostly attitude. You think things are messed up and you'll mostly be right."

They rode on, neither speaking, the ocean changing from purple to deep blue to bright blue, and they were side by side, Danny in the helm chair and his son standing beside him, as the first orange blaze of the sun suddenly appeared at the horizon.

"Out here you can sure see why they call it daybreak," Rick said.

"Yeah, or the crack of dawn," Danny replied. "It's a pretty sharp marker. Every dawn is a new beginning; every day you start from zero."

Rick looked at him and laughed. "You're awful profound today. Sun's up, and I better get to tying baits. I want you to show me that Chinese fingers knot again."

Rick worked more quickly this morning, and Danny noted that there was efficiency in his movements. Hell, I guess my attitude wasn't all that hot, either. I rode him too hard. He's trying to do better, and I should do the same.

A half-hour later Rick had finished his second daisy chain and had the mackerel laid out for the third. The southeast corner of Block Island was four miles off their starboard quarter, and he paused to look up at the deep shadows cast by the sun along its cliffs. "We're going to a different place," he yelled to Danny.

"Yeah, take a break. I'll show you the game plan," Danny yelled back.

Rick stood up, wiped his hands, and walked into the deckhouse.

"Go down below and bring up the chart," Danny said.

When Rick had laid the chart out on the console, Danny pointed to a spot on it and said, "There's where we were day before yesterday. But those fish appeared to be moving west." He moved his finger to the left on the chart. "If you follow in that direction, you get to this bank, where it goes from thirty-one fathoms to twenty-four. That's a moraine, left by the last glacier, all gravel, and it holds baitfish. Block Islanders used to call it 'the old tuna grounds,' and I'd like to have a dollar in the bank for every pound of fish I've taken off it over the years."

"So you figure they've gone there?"

"Either gone there or headin' there. We'll start there and work to where we were, in case I'm wrong. Maybe we'll ambush 'em instead of chasing 'em. Also, it's gonna blow later, out of the sou'west, and I'd rather be workin' with it than against it. Especially if you get to feelin' poorly." Danny was smirking at his last remark, but Rick ignored it.

A half-hour later, Danny slowed the boat to about eleven knots. Rick looked up. "I'm almost done," he said. "You ready to put 'em in?"

"Nah, I want to look around. We're just coming up on the north side of the bank, but I don't see much yet. I'm gonna work to the southeast corner, look for the bait. When you're done there you can go up in the tower."

Rick loved the tuna tower. Above the diesel throb it was quiet, and at searching speed the slower pitch and roll and the sound of water rushing along the hull reminded him of sailing and of his summer on a windjammer off the coast of Maine, a happy time in an unhappy childhood. There had been no seasickness; that only started later and only happened on fishing boats. His father had told him to scan the whole ocean, but that he should concentrate his search close, within a quarter-mile. But the sea drew his eyes outward, the horizon falling away all around, the sky a blue bowl with him in the center, at the masthead of a great frigate or a swift clipper ship.

He was Ishmael, at the masthead of the PEQUOD, searching the sea for the great white whale, and his eye caught a spout off in the distance ahead. He snapped back to reality thinking that he had imagined it but was startled by its vividness. And there it was again, this time for sure. "Whales!" he screamed out, and again, "Whales! Eleven o'clock!"

Danny was watching for baitfish on the recorder screen of the fishfinder when Rick yelled. He stepped out of the deckhouse and shouted back, "Put me on 'em, Rick. I can't see 'em from down here!" Then he strode back into the deckhouse, subtracted twelve degrees from the autopilot, and added two hundred rpm to the engine speed. As the boat settled onto its new course, Rick yelled, "You're on 'em. Hold her right there!"

Danny went back out on deck and yelled, "Still see 'em?"

Rick was leaning forward in the tower, his hand shading his eyes. "Yes! There's a bunch of 'em! I can see them rolling!"

Two minutes later Danny could see them from the deckhouse, and two minutes after that he began to mark bait, sand eels he figured, first scattered bunches and then clouds that showed on the screen from eighty feet almost to the surface. He slowed to trolling speed, shut off the autopilot, and yelled to Rick, "Pilot's off! You take it! Head into the whales. I'll put out the gear!"

Rick took the helm in the tower while Danny snapped daisy chains to the ends of the lines on each of the three big rods and began to feed them over the side, the first one farthest back and attached to the tag line on the port outrigger, the second closer and on the starboard rigger, and the third only a boat length from the transom and clipped to the center rigger. When he was satisfied that the presentation was perfect he climbed into the tower and checked them from above. "Calm day like this, they have to be perfect," he said to Rick.

"You want this?" Rick asked, stepping back from the steering wheel.

"No, you're doing fine. Work around the whales, look for fish. Lots of life here, Rick, and no other boats. They all went east. If the giants show up, we're gonna be heroes. If you see some, work in front of them. I'm going back down on deck. If we get a hookup, sing out, and I'll take it while you come down, but don't get so excited you break your neck."

But after two hours nothing had happened. There were still clouds of baitfish hanging to the edge of the bank, but the whales had moved southeast and were out of sight and the seabirds had settled down on the water in rafts. Danny climbed up into the tower and took the helm. He steered the boat into a large raft of shearwaters, forcing the birds to take off. "Get off your lazy asses and find me some tuna!" he yelled at them, and to Rick he said, "Patience isn't my long suit. Let's bring in the gear and head east and look for them."

An hour later they were both in the tower, intent in their search, neither speaking. A slight breeze had come up, making the ocean sparkle and giving the boat a gentle pitching motion. Rick went below to make a sandwich and to rest his eyes.

Off in the distance—he judged it at three miles—Danny

could see several boats moving slowly, apparently trolling. Watching them, he saw a wake, or rather what appeared to be a wake, at about a half-mile. But there were no boats that could have produced it. The wake changed shape, became circular, now several smaller wakes, moving westward, toward them. "Rick, we found 'em!" He shouted.

Rick came running out of the deckhouse. "Where?" he shouted back. Danny was pointing ahead. Rick started up the ladder, saw the commotion on the water, and stopped. "That's giants?" he asked.

"Sure is," Danny said. They were closing fast, and Danny brought the engine speed down to idle.

"I'll put out the gear!" Rick said.

"No hurry," Danny replied. "Come up here; I want you to see this."

Rick climbed the rest of the way into the tower, and they watched as the wake turned into several acres of dancing, nervous water, growing darker as it approached, then with flashes of white and silver, finally resolving into separate dark masses that were giant bluefin tuna. Danny circled the school and slowly angled into it, and suddenly they were surrounded by huge bodies that seemed to Rick to be the size of small automobiles. He watched them swimming along, porpoising up and down without effort, a dorsal fin and broad back cutting the surface, gliding down fifteen feet or so, then a quick thrust back to the surface, the fish sometimes rolling onto its side and sometimes rolling completely over, its belly suddenly stark white against the dark water and the even darker backs of the others. Individual fish seemed playful, but as he looked out across the whole school he sensed enormous subdued power, a majestic force, on its own mission, subject only to its own whim.

"You're a hunter, Rick, looking at the last buffalo."

"The last buffalo?" The simile was evident—wide and lonely, the rolling sea and the rolling prairie, anachronistic men on an atavistic pursuit, grasping for the last shreds of a glory already passed—but Rick wanted to hear the story.

"Yes," Danny said, speaking softly, "I remember, and it was only twenty years ago, schools ten times bigger than this, all up and down the sound, up in the mouth of Narragansett Bay, all along the south shore. Hell, in the summertime you could drive along the shore from Westerly to Narragansett and stop on any high ground with binoculars and see them. Ten minutes from the dock and you were fishing for them. Now we've got to come way out here, thirty miles offshore, to find this one little school."

"How did it happen so fast?" Rick asked.

"Same as the buffalo. A fad market with too much money. What did the buffalo was the Sharps rifle and the railroad. What did the giant tuna was the purse seine."

"What about you? You sell them."

Danny hesitated, but he detected no accusation in the boy's question, although when he spoke his voice was harder and had risen, "I'm no saint, Rick, and there's not much difference between me and the purse seiner except that my methods aren't likely to kill them all. I just wish the price hadn't gone so high. Or they'd outlaw exporting them. Then we could all go back to being sportsmen."

"And lose all the money?"

"If we'd never had it we wouldn't miss it. It's almost gone now anyway. Some of the guys up on Cape Cod think the ocean's still full of giants 'cause they still see a lot, but it's the last place left, like the last big herd of buffalo. No, Rick, we sold the house and blew the money on a big party, and the hangover's gonna be a bitch. If we stop screwing up maybe you might live long enough to see them come back—but I won't."

They had dropped back and were now behind the school, still rolling and ambling along to the west. Danny added a hundred rpm to keep up with them. "I'd like my grandchildren to be able to see some of what I have," he said.

"Aren't you kind of counting your chickens early?" Rick asked. "Where's all this family coming from? I'm going to college this year."

"Hell, as horny as you are? And that pretty blonde girl-friend? Won't be long, I'll have a passel of grandkids."

"You don't know what you're talking about!"

"Ha! You were out with her Sunday night, and Monday morning while you were still asleep, I walked by your car to get in my truck, and I couldn't help but notice a pair of panties on the back seat."

Rick's ears and cheeks flushed. Danny, smirking, looked at him and said, "I like that red better than the green."

"You're a dirty old man," Rick replied. "Are we gonna catch one of these buffaloes or not?"

"There's no real hurry. They're not feeding now anyway. Though I suppose they could start anytime. I'll circle around in front of 'em and then you can put the gear out."

Rick retreated from the tower, and Danny idled the engine until all of the fish had passed, then speeded up and turned to circle south of them while Rick took the daisy chains out of the coolers, snapped them on the lines, and laid them on the gunwales. When he was ahead of the leading fish, Danny slowed to match their speed, then nodded to Rick, who was standing by the port rig looking up at him. Rick lowered the rig into the water and let it run back, then looked up at Danny before attaching it to the tagline. "How's that?" he yelled.

"Too far. Bring it in three turns . . . right there. Tag it."

When all three lines were set Danny slowed the diesel and soon the school overtook them, giant tuna rolling by on both sides, the whole school passing without showing any interest in their baits. Danny speeded up a hundred rpm and moved back through the school, the baits now moving faster than the fish. He zigzagged, trying to trigger a strike, but nothing happened, and soon they were ahead of the school again. Rick had climbed halfway up the tower. "They don't want to play," he said.

"We're almost back where we started," Danny replied, "Maybe they'll turn on when they hit all that baitfish."

But a half-mile from the bank the entire school sounded, and Rick said, "Where'd they go?"

"Deep out of sight. I'm not sure, but I think we'd better move up onto the bank." Danny increased the speed as much as he dared without tearing up the soft bodies of the trolled mackerel and headed straight west. A hundred yards from the edge of the bank he saw showers of baitfish jumping clear of the water ahead.

"Look at that," Rick said.

"Somethin's sure pushing them," Danny replied, "Might be our tuna. Let's get down on deck."

Danny took the helm at the after station and turned northwest, into the thick of the baitfish. Rick was next to him but facing aft, and he was watching when the two inside daisy chains were engulfed in grenadelike explosions, the tagline releases snapping like pistol shots, the rods bent hard over, both reels screaming. "Fish on!" he screamed and jumped to the empty rod, spinning the handle, not knowing what they would do with two giant tuna on at once, but knowing that he first had to clear this one out of the way.

Danny turned the boat sixty degrees to starboard and dropped to idle speed. He saw that the lines to the two fish were crossed and that the center line was underneath so he decided to crank up the drag and pop that fish off. His hand was on the lever, pushing forward, when the other rod snapped up, the line slack. He pulled the lever back and jumped to the other rod, yanked it out of the holder, and flipped the slack line over the one with the fish before they could tangle. He handed the rod to Rick, now back next to him, and said, "Crank this in quick, I've gotta turn the boat!" Rick dropped the rod tip and spun the handle, and by the time Danny had the boat turned to put the fish off the starboard quarter the rigs were clear and Rick was climbing into the fighting chair.

Danny ran to the rod, jammed tight in the holder, backed the drag off, and wrestled it out and over to the chair. He pushed the rod butt into the gimbal and forced it up so Rick could snap the harness into the lugs on the top of the reel. "You know what we have to do," he said, "Now let's *do it*!"

"Yeah!" Rick shouted.

"Let's get some line back," Danny said. "I'm turning to starboard. Crank hard as soon as you can! I want to fight this fish *close*!" He brought the boat around and followed the fish, now slowing from his first frantic run, and Rick recovered most of the line before the fish took off again.

"How does he feel?" Danny asked.

"This is a big fish, Dad. Did you see the explosion when he hit? I saw him! I saw him when he took it!"

"Good. Then you know what you're up against. Keep the pressure constant, and if nothing breaks we'll get him," Danny was watching the line, still running out, but more slowly. "He's going to the right. I'm gonna back around and turn the boat."

The fish made two more runs, then went deep and pulled steadily southwest. Danny followed, keeping the fish off the starboard quarter, Rick pulling to keep his head turned, wear him down. He would slide forward in the seat, getting a half-turn of line onto the reel, pumping back with his legs, then the fish would spurt forward and take it back. Danny concentrated on the line, maintaining its angle with little course corrections. He shifted his gaze, watched his son. He said he wasn't ready. Christ, before this is over I'm going to believe in ghosts. So long ago, and the world so different. Danny had been a boy on a farm in Maine, younger than his own son was now, and he had wanted to hunt deer like the men, bring one home to hang in the barn and feed the family, and his grandfather had taught him about rifles and hunting and had taken him to the mountain, and in the afternoon of that first day they had jumped a forkhorn and Danny had watched it running, a clear shot but he forgot to bring the rifle up until it was too late so he snapped the shot and missed. Afterwards he told his grandfather that it wasn't buck fever, it was just that he hadn't been ready for it to be a deer. His grandfather had smiled and said something that Danny couldn't now remember, something about having missed a few himself, but he remembered the smile because the old man had a Yankee sense of humor and almost never smiled.

"He's shaking his head!"

Danny's eyes snapped to the rod tip, bouncing up and down by a foot or more. "Relax, Rick," he said. "Lower the tip when he does that so he can't get any slack, and keep the pressure constant. Remember what I said about a strong hand with a gentle touch. Like making love to a woman."

"Everything with you gets down to that, doesn't it?"

"Kid, everything in life gets down to that sooner or later."

A half-hour later the fish made another run, but the line arced up, and suddenly he surfaced, a hundred yards away, his tail thrashing the water white. He circled slowly to the right, directly off the transom, and began to pull the boat slowly backward, although line was still going out. "Run the drag up halfway to full," Danny said. "Pulling the boat on the surface like this, he'll kill himself in ten minutes."

But ten minutes later the fish was still on the surface, and although his tail thrashed more slowly, the strokes were powerful, and he showed no sign of weakening. Another twenty minutes passed, and still the fish was on the surface, pulling the boat slowly backward.

"I think my watch stopped," Rick said.

"What?"

"You said he'd be all done in ten minutes, so I figure my watch must have stopped."

"You smartass, I hope he pulls your arms out of their sockets," Danny smiled, but his gaze was on the fish. "I've never seen one do this for so long, Rick. This is a very strong fish. Very big, too, and in his prime."

"Yeah, well so am I," Rick said, and then, more softly, "as long as we don't break him off."

The fish finally sounded, then turned and ran straight at them. Danny pushed the throttle all the way forward, and black diesel smoke poured from the exhaust as he spun the boat to the right, shouting, "Reel . . . reel . . . reel," and they circled the hissing line before it could pass under the boat. "Just like bull-fighting!" Danny said, his eyes bright.

"That was slick," Rick said. He was leaning back in the chair, his legs straight against the footrest, his arms down, the fish pulling line straight out, but slowly now. "He's tiring."

"How are you doing?" Danny asked.

"I'm fine," Rick replied.

"Looks like you worked a few things out from the other day."

"I did a lot of thinking, Dad."

"Yeah, me too, kid."

The fish circled to the left and stopped taking line. Danny ran parallel to him, moving slowly closer, as Rick gained line. "We've got almost three hours on this fish," Danny said. "Let's see if he's ready to take. Push the drag up."

Rick forced the fish up about fifty feet, pumping and reeling, then felt him surge forward and could bring him no closer, although he didn't lose any line. The standoff continued, the fish a hundred feet down and swimming straight, the boat running with him. Rick could feel him twisting, no longer a head shake, but more a writhing of the whole body, trying to get free. Rick wanted it to be over, and he pulled harder, panting now, his lips pulled back, and Danny could hear a low growl in his throat when he exhaled.

Suddenly the line arced upward, and the pointed nose of the fish broke the surface less than a hundred feet from them. He rolled and dove to thirty feet, but Danny could see the white flash of his sides. "This is the dénouement, kid. Hold him while I get ready."

When the lance, the meathook, and the tailropes were in place, Danny asked, "Want me to go over it?"

"No," Rick said. "I'm all set."

"Okay. Just remember to back off the drag halfway when I stick him, so we can get a second chance if I screw up." Rick nodded his head.

Danny shifted to neutral, and the fish moved under the starboard quarter, sixty feet down and circling counterclockwise. Rick used the circles to gain line, reeling in when the fish circled closer, holding the line from going out when he circled away. Danny stood next to the rod tip, staring down into the water. "I see him. He's on his side. Keep it smooooth." He picked up the lance, his left hand holding the shaft, his right cupped over the end, and moved to the right side of the line. The fish was less than thirty feet down; Danny could see the hook, and he felt the sudden grip of dread. "He's not hooked good, Rick! Any slack and we'll lose this one too!" Rick pressed his lips together and stared at the rod tip, held it steady, and slowly gained line.

"Next turn and I'll take him when he passes the transom!" The line circled away, then closer, closer, and the fish was on his side, ten feet away, and Danny leaned, his body tense as a loaded spring, and as he lunged the fish snapped upright and surged away, the dart skidding along the top of his head.

"I missed!" Danny screamed as he pulled the lance back into the boat, away from the line. But Rick was staring away where the fish had stopped, and he kept hard pressure, forcing the exhausted giant to turn, his nose out of the water, and roll back on his side.

Danny dropped the lance and ran to reposition the boat, his heart hammering. "I wouldn't have believed he could do that! I've never seen one this strong!" Danny had seen the hook as the fish passed, was sure that he would get no more than one more shot, if he even got that.

The fish circled twice more before he was close enough, and Danny said, "This time is it!" and the position was exactly the same and again the fish tried to snap upright but Danny aimed a little lower and felt the dart go in, but the fish was surging away, and the shaft of the lance hit the leader and the hook pulled free, and Danny roared and dove forward, driving the shaft with his outstretched right hand, and Rick was out of the fighting chair and had him by the legs as he went over the side.

"It's not in good!" Danny yelled as Rick pulled him into the boat. "Get the meathook. I'll pull him up!" Danny pulled on the dart line, slowly drawing the huge fish toward him. Rick stood next to him, the meathook in his hand. "We only got him on this one line. Reach over the top of him and put it in his eye, drive it right into his brain!" Rick could see that the dart was planted very deeply, but Danny was in a fury, so he said nothing as he set the meathook and pulled up hard. "Take both lines . . . bring him alongside . . . I'll tailrope him . . . you don't own him 'til he's tailroped!" But Rick was already smiling as Danny looped the rope around the fish's tail, tied it to the quarter cleat, and threw his two clenched fists into the air with a howl. Then he turned to his son, and they threw their arms around each other.

"You got him! You got your first giant!" Danny was in an ecstasy of arm waving and hand pumping.

"What the hell were you gonna do, jump in and strangle him?"

"You had hold of me!"

Rick shook his head, laughing, "You're crazy!"

"Kid, there was no way I was gonna lose that fish! Look at him! He'll go over seven hundred pounds!"

"Well, we got him! We really got him!" Rick leaned over the side, looked at the enormous mass of the giant tuna, quivering in death, and all at once a wave of sadness passed through him.

Danny shifted the boat into gear and idled along with the autopilot set on a northerly course. He drew his belt knife, leaned over the fish, and made a quick stab on each side, just behind the pectoral fins, severing the lateral arteries.

The breeze was increasing, and they stood there, now silent, looking down at the fish, the side of the boat and the fish plunging into the rising seas, now washing over the broad black back, carrying away swirls of blood from his sides. Danny thought of Mel. He would call her on the way in to arrange for a buyer to meet them. Rick was thinking that he was very glad that he had hunted and killed this grand fish and that he was very sure that he would not do it again.

CHAPTER 9

Billfish; Tournaments; Addiction and Atavism

Persephone, fulfill my wish,
And grant that in the shades below
My ghost may land the ghosts of fish!
—Andrew Lang, *Angling Sketches,* 1890

I object to fishing tournaments less for what they do to fish than
what they do to fishermen. I would not argue that fish tourneys
should be banned, just that they be recognized for what they
are—distractions from what's truly important.
—Ted Williams, *Fishing to Win,* 1984

If there is a heaven, and I am allowed past the pearly gates, I
wish to spend eternity chasing white marlin across celestial
seas. But I fear that simple justice will point me in the other direction with white marlin, bills slashing at my naked buttocks, forever chasing me across flaming brimstone. They are beautiful fish!
Of all the fish that swim the ocean, I am most entranced by white
marlin.

While to my mind the white marlin is unique, in fact it is
just one of several billfish, and not the largest either. The Atlantic
also holds sailfish, blue marlin, and swordfish, as well as the
smaller and more rarely seen spearfish.

The sailfish is everyman's billfish—abundant, accessible even to small boaters within sight of shore, and rather easy to catch. Sailfish have been taken as far north as Cape Cod, although they are rare north of Cape Hatteras. South of Cape Hatteras they are the offshore fish most sought by anglers, and they are staples of the Florida charterboat fleet. Even tourists and occasional anglers catch them, and I am certain that the number of sailfish that have been taken by rod and reel far exceeds the total for all other billfish combined.

If sailfish are seen as the most egalitarian of billfish, blue marlin occupy the other end of the social spectrum. The locations where they're found and the boat lines their seekers seem to prefer reek of status: Bimini, Walker's Cay, Eleuthera; Bertram, Rybovich, Hatteras—names that bespeak big, fast sport-fishing yachts and high rollers with fat wallets and a thirst for expensive adventure in opulent tropical settings. It costs a lot of money to fish for blue marlin. But occasionally one is taken off southern New England, although almost always outside of the forty-fathom line and almost always by accident while trolling for tuna. These New England blue marlin are large fish, mostly over five hundred pounds, females wandering northward with the Gulf Stream. I once hooked one on light tackle while fishing for small yellowfin tuna south of Martha's Vineyard, but broke it off after a minute or two. The huge fish struck with no warning, caused brief pandemonium, and left stunned silence when she snapped the leader and departed.

Swordfish are a New England tragedy. Late in the spring of every year since the last ice age they would swarm onto the outer half of the continental shelf, from the New York Bight to the far reaches of Georges Bank, and in late autumn return to wherever they had come from. Harpooners began taking them at least as far back as the early nineteenth century, and by early twentieth century a successful commercial harpoon fishery for them had been developed, followed after World War I by a limited rod-and-reel sportfishery. The total harvest during those years averaged around a thousand tons per year, which proved sustainable, especially since both methods targeted only the largest fish and were inefficient, at least by the standards of later industrial fishing. But by the late sixties and early seventies the pelagic longline, miles long and with thousands of hooks that take all sizes of fish, had become the predominant method of commercial harvest, and catches multiplied more than ten times.

The exact numbers of swordfish taken and swordfish remaining are vehemently argued among groups with various agendas, but the plain fact is that thirty years ago it was not uncommon to see a dozen swordfish in a day offshore, but now it has been more than a decade since I have seen a single one. During his career as a charterboat captain, Bob Linton was able to catch fifty-four swordfish on rod and reel, thirteen of which were taken in 1963 alone, but now it has been more than a decade and a half since I have heard of an angler anywhere off New England catching even one. Swordfish are still found in other parts of the world, but on our continental shelf the swordfish is as good as extinct. I still see "Block Island swordfish" on restaurant menus, but that description is a sad and bitter little lie, because it has been years since a swordfish was landed at Block Island or anywhere in the adjacent waters.

By default, then, the white marlin remains as the only viable Yankee billfishery—although that is hardly the source of my fascination. The white marlin is a unique fish, and his old sobriquet "king of the light-tackle offshore gamefish" was well earned. I have wandered a lot of ocean looking for white marlin and have spent a lot of time trying to entice them, but I have caught precious few compared with my score on other offshore species. White marlin are not for the beginning angler or the dilettante. Catching them requires knowledge of the ocean, skill in seamanship and offshore angling technique, and endless patience.

White marlin are unpredictable and surrounded by mystery. We know next to nothing about the species. They seem to breed in the spring, since spent roe sacs are found in females in early summer, but no one knows where or under what conditions. They are found alone or in groups of two or three but are never seen in schools, although food abundance and ocean currents may concentrate many of them in a particular area. Little is known of their migration, but the continental shelf off southern New England seems to be the northern edge of their range. In warmer years we may have a lot of them while in cooler years we may have very few.

White marlin are sometimes wary and sometimes indifferent, but they feed aggressively and often demonstrate a quick and violent temper, which can be the key to catching them. A marlin feeds by attacking a school of baitfish, cutting out a bunch of them the way a quarter horse works cattle on a roundup, and driving them to the surface, spinning around to ball them up into a tight cluster, then slashing, stunning, and killing them with his bill. The early Yankee fishermen, many of whom hailed from Scotland, likened this spinning behavior of feeding white marlin to a highland dance called the skillyghillie and called the marlin "skilly," a name still occasionally heard in New England.

A skillying white marlin can be seen from a long way off, either by the surface commotion or the seabirds attracted to an easy feed on stunned and broken baitfish. This is when a marlin is most vulnerable to an angler with any small live bait. The technique is to dash up to within casting range of the feeding marlin, preferably with the sun behind you, and lob your bait into the melee. If you are quick enough, and can place the bait right in front of his nose, he may grab it. Or he may simply smash it to pieces with his bill and never get the hook in his mouth. If he grabs the bait while turning and you simultaneously reel up the slack, you may be able to set the hook in the soft corner of his mouth.

Or, if your lob cast doesn't leave enough slack, or he doesn't turn, the bait may simply be yanked out of his mouth, the hook sliding harmlessly along his hard bill.

When not in feeding mode, white marlin are often seen cruising along on the surface, lazily riding the waves downsea, black scimitar tails standing straight up and hardly moving. This is when they can be most maddening. To get a strike, the angler must first engage the fish's attention, then either put him into a feeding mode or anger him (or a little of both), and then get him to grab something with a hook in it. The technique is called "teasing," although I am not sure if it is the marlin or the angler who is being most teased.

The first step in teasing a white marlin is to put from one to four splashy surface lures or baits in a group seventy feet or so behind the boat and then maneuver them in front of the lazily moving fish. Once in a blue moon he quickly attacks one, but mostly he simply ignores them. The idea is to keep passing them in front of him until he takes an interest, usually signaled by speeding up to look them over, perhaps even rapping one with his bill. When he does this, you must pull it away from him, the obvious escape movement piquing his interest still further. After several times, when he is quivering with excitement and the luminescent stripes along his sides are "lit up," it is time to yank the teaser completely out of the water and instantly replace it with a rigged ballyhoo or other baitfish. If your judgment is correct and your timing is perfect, he charges the bait and engulfs it in a slashing attack. With just the right dropback to allow his head to turn and a quick hookset, you are on!

Mostly, though, it doesn't go this way, and the white marlin simply ignores the teasers. Or he may sink down and disappear, perhaps resurfacing some distance away. At this point, you sometimes can trigger a strike by maneuvering the boat behind him, with a spread of surface lures out, and then running right over him. You won't actually hit him, but he will skitter downward, obviously startled. This is where the famous white marlin temper comes in. When he gets down a few yards anger takes over and he may come back to the surface, lit up and ready to kill whatever disturbed him, and if the lures are passing over at just the right moment he may charge them like an angry bull.

There is a lot of contingency in all of this and more than a bit of luck. But luck follows skill and experience, both of which come from study and practice. All truly great fishing requires a marriage of luck with skill. Bob Linton used to say that for every fifty white marlin you see, you might get four to charge a bait and one solid hookup. You have to be very, very skilled to exceed this ratio.

The payoff for all of the time, effort, and red-eyed frustration is, of course, that one solid hookup. The white marlin's anger explodes when he feels the hook, and he takes off in a series of jumps, pirouettes, and hard runs, greyhounding away one minute, circling back the next, testing the angler's skill at controlling drag, slack, and his own hammering heart. The white marlin's power is much different than a tuna's. The tuna is a slugger, a heavy-hitting John L. Sullivan—relentless and dogged. The white marlin is a boxer, a quick-stepping Gentleman Jim Corbett—sophisticated and tricky.

But there is something else about a white marlin. Being joined to one is to touch an ancient and mystic force. Part of this feeling may be that we know so little about them and part may be that they are so wild and uncontrollable, but I think there is more to it. There is magic in a white marlin, and an encounter with one—win or lose—leaves you dry-mouthed and shaky.

As with so many other species, their numbers are now being depleted by the forces of industrial fishing. White marlin are not even the target, but only an unintended bycatch of the indiscriminate longline, a travesty that also depletes the human spirit.

The white marlin is a perfect hunter: strong but lonely, fearless but a bit insolent, noble but quick-tempered. I have been told that assigning such anthropomorphic descriptions to a mere fish is unrealistic, and I know that is true, although I don't really believe it. The romantic in me isn't quite dead yet.

• • •

I am ambivalent toward fishing tournaments, because my experiences with them have encompassed fun-filled festivals spiced with friendly competition as well as nasty ego trips filled with cheating and rancor. There doesn't seem to be a middle ground. Each tournament takes on a personality that is either joyous or malevolent, depending on such elements as its organization, location, constituency, and even the market value of the target fish species.

All tournaments also have a life cycle. The regular contestants grow older and richer and buy bigger boats, and the character of the tournament changes. Then, through death or declining health, they are replaced by young people with much smaller boats and different values, and the character of the tournament changes again. The Block Island Billfish Invitational Tournament went through such an evolution over a three-decade period that also coincided with a relentless decline in the billfishery as well as explosive growth and change in the character of the Block Island community. I used to love that tournament, and I guess it is still a pretty good one, but I no longer participate in it. It has become so different from the tournaments of my recollection that I prefer to keep the memory intact.

Many saltwater fishing tournaments that began as topnotch events at some point in their history succumbed to a decline in the targeted fishery. This happened in the seventies to most of the fine old striped bass tournaments, although the recovery in the striper fishery over the past few years has reenergized local fishing

clubs, and new, still mostly small, striper tournaments are spring-
ing up like mushrooms after an autumn rain.

A unique case of tournament decline occurred with giant
bluefin tuna. The integrity of every tournament directed at giant
tuna was actually destroyed before the stocks collapsed. The steep
increase in the dockside value of a dead giant tuna in the late seventies became a corrosive influence, and widespread gold-rush
fever first blurred, then dissolved, the distinction between sport
fishing for tournament points and commercial fishing for profit.
Cheating and rancorous conflict became so commonplace that
when the fish were finally gone, the soul of the tournaments had
become so rotten that their subsequent death was just a mercy
killing.

The situation had gotten so bad by the mid-eighties that
I ceased entering any tuna tournaments, and even if the stocks
should recover sometime in the future, there is little chance that
I will change my mind. The final straw came when the organizers of a major tournament, one that I had enjoyed for several
years, changed the tournament dates at the last minute to a time
three weeks later for the sole purpose of trying to catch the market for the fish at a higher price. When I pointed out that not
only did this reasoning violate the concept of fishing for sport,
but that three of the vessels entered, including my own, were
charterboats whose customers were locked in to the originally
scheduled dates, the answer I received was, "Screw the charterboats. You're outvoted." I angrily withdrew from the tournament and later felt a perverse joy when a high commercial
harvest forced the closure of the fishery a day before the start of
the new dates.

Actually, it didn't take much inducement for me to with-
draw, since by then I had about had it with tuna tournaments. The
idea behind a tournament is fair competition, with all competitors
sharing an equal balance between advantage and disadvantage
through agreed-upon rules of fair chase. But many captains and

anglers had been sneaking harpoons aboard, surreptitiously switching to heavy lines, and putting baits in the water before the starting time. It wasn't so much an intention to cheat in the tournament as it was an unwillingness to risk the loss of a fish worth thousands of dollars, but the result was the same. I remember entering one tournament where a winner was disqualified because it was found that the fish had been harpooned before it was gaffed, and another time I watched the mate on another boat participating in a tournament I hadn't entered, handline a fish while the angler simply wound the slack line onto the reel. Such incidents caused those who chose to play by the rules to become embittered, conflicts multiplied, and I just became flat-out disgusted by the whole mess.

The giant bluefin tuna situation was unique, and there are still some fine tournaments for other species. Successful fishing tournaments all share a set of common characteristics. First, they are relaxed, well organized, and efficiently run. There may be some scurrying about to make it all work, but this behind-the-scenes work is never evident to the contestants. Captains' meetings, cookouts, banquets, and awards ceremonies occur on time and as advertised. Second, they are conducted from attractive areas that people visit with their families even when they aren't in a tournament. Third, conflicts are minimized by having clear, sensible rules that are equally enforced. Fourth, the desired constituency is targeted through selected advertising and accurate promotional literature, and cohesion is maintained by restricting the number of boats and arranging for them to be berthed together. Crummy tournaments get that way when the organizers ignore these common-sense procedures.

Every good tournament has a central organizing principle, a *raison d'être*. It may be dedicated to a particular species, such as white marlin, or a group of species, such as billfish, or a particular type of tackle or bait, or a particular type of boat, or it may be dedicated to a particular charity or cause to which all or a portion of the proceeds are donated. Many of the very best tournaments are combinations, such as a light-tackle billfish tournament to benefit a local charity or a youth bluefish tournament to fund a teen drug program.

Whatever their other pros and cons, many saltwater fishing tournaments have been valuable to fisheries science. Historic tournament records going back a century or more have been valuable in tracking the population trends of several species, and modern fisheries biologists regularly use tournaments to aid population and migration studies as well as to get tissue samples for research on such subjects as fish genetics and physiology.

Shark tournaments have been particularly valuable in this regard, and the scientists of now-retired Dr. Jack Casey's Apex Predator Investigation have been making the circuit of Atlantic coast shark tournaments for almost four decades. Important as is the understanding of shark biology that has come from this program, there is another understanding that may be of greater importance in the long run. The program begun by Jack Casey has promoted mutual respect between scientists and fishermen, two groups who haven't always gotten along well, but who have to cooperate if we are to restore and protect our fisheries. Biology can explain what we have, but can't save it—only intelligent conservation policy, based on good science but set in the political arena, can do that. Respect for science by both anglers and commercial fishermen as well as respect for fishermen by scientists is necessary to make it work.

All is not bleak. While the National Marine Fisheries Service has been filling its ranks with what John Steinbeck called "dry-ball" biologists, several states have employed the real ones. Massachusetts has Greg Skomal and Brad Chase, two young biologists cut from the same cloth as Steinbeck's Monterey acquaintance "Doc" Ed Ricketts and the old-time naturalists. These are people who know how to run a boat or repair a balky engine. They are not afraid of fish blood on their clothes or dirt on their hands, and they know how to have a good time. They also listen to fishermen, are not afraid to tell the truth, and on top of that they are very good scientists. If they want to know the effect of a certain hook type on fish, they find out how it is used, design a controlled experiment, and get the answer. If they want to know the effect of prolonged battle on bluefin tuna, they catch some and subject them to controlled stress while measuring such indicators as blood gases, lactic acid buildup, recovery times, and survival rates, and they get the answer.

One project Greg and Brad are responsible for is the Massachusetts Sportfishing Tournament Monitoring Program, which began in 1987 and has covered 100 percent of the state's big-game fishing tournaments since 1990. Their faces have become familiar on the docks, where they are well liked and universally respected. Their well-written annual reports on trends in tournament success rates, overall efforts, and catch per unit effort, covering a dozen species, have become a valuable chronicle of the generally declining health of the East Coast offshore fisheries.

• • •

Recently there have been a number of printed criticisms of fishing tournaments that have seemed to me to be mostly off the mark. The more serious criticism comes from those who regard fishing as a solitary sport, perhaps even as an atavistic ritual, a throwback to our hunter-gatherer roots. The solitary sport part I can agree with, at least as it applies to fly fishing on a mountain stream or surf casting on a lonely stretch of beach. The atavistic ritual part I once agreed with, and still do, sort of, although less so as I have matured. Keith McCafferty, one of my favorite outdoor writers, has written that in hunting and fishing we "reach toward an ancient pulse," and that is true, as far as it goes. But he also says "worlds have to be bridged," and that is equally true. It is a long, long way from the world of a well-fed and impeccably equipped modern angler to the world of a Stone Age hunter-gatherer. There may be a line from one to the other, but it is tenuous at best, particularly when the angler is fifty miles out to sea on a diesel-powered, electronically navigated, and very expensive offshore sportfisherman. As for solitude, off-shore fishing is a team sport—aggressive, at times even boister-ous. Come to think of it, maybe there is a line that stretches all the way back from a team of offshore tournament anglers in competition with other boats to a group of hunter-gatherers in competition with other tribes. It's just that their stakes were so very much higher back then.

Yet, there *is* something special about fishing, and it applies at least equally to the other blood sport, hunting. Both fishing and hunting can be enormously satisfying in a way that is hard to de-scribe, although generations of writers and artists from many cul-tures have tried to do so. Perhaps what they have sought to touch really is an "ancient pulse," but I am reluctant to call upon genetic memory to explain it.

There is another possible explanation. B. F. Skinner, the famous and controversial experimental psychologist, showed that many behavioral responses are learned through a process he called "operant conditioning." Basically, operant conditioning is the con-tinuous input of both reward and pain to either imprint or extin-guish any particular behavior or group of behaviors. Skinner found that the most strongly imprinted behaviors are produced when the reward is on an intermittent and unpredictable schedule, a cir-cumstance that exactly describes both fishing and hunting and that offers one possible explanation of why these pursuits can become so addictive.

Both fishing and hunting can be satisfying in a way that is akin to the equally ancient pulse of sex, but is this instinctive? They can also be addictive in a way that is akin to a laboratory animal tripping a switch for a food pellet, but is this conditioned? Are fishing and hunting atavistic rituals based upon tribal memory, or are they behavioral responses based upon operant conditioning? Maybe the truth lies somewhere in between, but I, for one, hope we never discover it.

CHAPTER 10

The Tuna Tower; How to Catch a Fish;
Offshore Fishing; The Edge of the Shelf

"I envy not him that eats better meat than I do, nor him that
is richer, or that wears better clothes than I do. I envy no body
but him, and him only, that catches more fish than I do."
—Izaak Walton, *The Compleat Angler,* 1653

Once you are out of sight of land and of the other boats
you are more alone than you can ever be hunting and the
sea is the same as it has been since before men ever went
on it in boats.
—Ernest Hemingway, *On the Blue Water,* 1936

The tuna tower is most certainly going to bring about my ultimate demise. I know this with a degree of certainty, yet I do nothing about it. In this regard I am no different from the confirmed smoker who, despite constant hoarseness and a heavy chronic cough, yet continues the habit, even to the point of awakening in the middle of the night in an attack of hacking to have another cigarette. Or the alcoholic who, despite memory loss and a cirrhotic liver, won't begin the day without an eye-opener or finish it sober. In my case the agent of my fate will be neither emphysema nor cirrhosis but melanoma.

Like the smoker and the drinker, I know where the danger lies, but choose to ignore it. There are occasional moments, particularly in the heat of a calm midsummer day with the bright light dancing on the ocean and into my eyes, when the reality of the sun's power penetrates my consciousness, and I briefly shudder at the memory of the manner of death of someone I knew well who succumbed to that horrible disease. But the moment quickly passes, and the memory recedes into the joy of the tower. I am alone, free, and on top of the world.

On top of the world. I guess that really is the defining sensation. With no land in sight there is nothing of the solid earth above the level of my eyes, and in the knowledge of a round earth, I see its curvature fall away in every direction. I clear my mind of thought, and there it is—I really *am* standing on the very top of it—the *whole* globe is beneath my feet. I know it is always true, but here I can *see* it and I can *feel* it. Then I look into the sky, sense the thinness of the atmosphere and the vastness beyond, and feel the motion of the sea, and I know the tight boundaries that surround my life. I may be lord of my realm, but my realm is very, very small. I think of the mice who live in the shed that I built who believe that the shed belongs to them and that I am the interloper.

Coming in from offshore, scanning the horizon for the first glimpse of Block Island's cliff tops on the horizon, I imagine the crow's nest high on the mast of the SANTA MARIA. Handling the sails or working on deck gave her crew no opportunity for introspection, but what of the lonely hours aloft, on watch, searching the sea? Surely someone must have known that sensation that I now feel. Did all of Columbus's men take a turn up there? Was there truly surprise at the final cry of "Land ho!" or only relief that the end of a long voyage was in sight?

Introspection, of course, isn't the purpose for which tuna towers are put on boats. Their primary function is to find fish by improving your ability to see, both outward and downward. That they should do this well makes sense. Vision outward is far greater from the tower because the curvature of the round earth restricts your horizon the closer you are to it—get up twenty or thirty feet and the distance you can see is multiplied several times over in every direction. Vision downward into the ocean is far greater because the angle of reflected light rays blocks your vision into the water the closer you are to it—get up twenty or thirty feet and the depth to which you can see is restricted mostly by plankton.

All of this is very sensible, but the effect is stunning. The first time I ever climbed into a tuna tower at sea, many years ago after an all-night drinking binge on Block Island, I was mostly looking for clear air for my howling head. What I found was a world that years on the ocean in small boats had never revealed to me. I saw whales blowing and rolling, basking sharks breaching, porpoises playing, marlin tailing, tuna jumping, and a swordfish finning on the surface. Within seventy feet of the boat I saw a marlin under the surface, several sea turtles, schools of bluefish skittering away from our passage, large sharks, giant ocean sunfish, and a jellyfish that must have been five feet across. Almost none of these creatures was visible from the deck, and I later heard at least one person remark on how dead the ocean seemed. Since that long-ago summer day I have seen many people climb into a tuna tower for the first time, and the effect is always the same—they always say something like, "*Wow!* You can see *forever!*"

Some offshore sport-fishing boats are designed with an enclosed bridge, some with both a bridge and a tuna tower, and some with just a tower. Both are for improved visibility, but the effect is far different. A tower frees you from the boundaries of the boat; a bridge only isolates you from the people in it. On the bridge you are remote, unreachable, above the people on the deck below. A bridge appeals to those who relish the role of captain. But it in no way brings you closer to the ocean around you—enclosure and electronic gadgets, in fact, give quite the opposite effect. In a tower, on the other hand, you are projected not so much above the boat as beyond it. You are a sensory organ, an extension of the boat into the sea and therefore an integral part of both. A visitor to the bridge may be greeted by its occupant in a somewhat imperious manner. A visitor to the tower is welcomed into the childlike world of constant discovery.

During the span of a year on the EARLY BIRD my charters include several hundred people. How each responds to the tower mirrors how each responds to life. Children and young adolescents are drawn to it, scamper up the ladder even before we leave the dock, ride the tower all day. The meat fishermen, mostly male, take their pleasure in filling their coolers, relishing the essential role of provider. Feet firmly planted on the deck, they take no notice of the tower unless it is to lean against one of its legs. The yuppie types, self-indulgent but seeing themselves as practical to a fault, only climb into the tower (wearing a wide-brimmed hat and lathered in sunscreen) when it is time to look for fish. On the way out they discuss such things as hook styles, fly-rod modulus, SPF factors, computers, and electronic navigation.

Then there are the dreamers, those who have never lost some essential part of childhood. Like the children, they too are drawn to the tower, although less as a novelty and more for its freedom from the confines of a boat and for its link to the pulse of the sea. Of all the people I meet it is these last I am most drawn to. They are the ones who hear the music and feel the poetry. They ride the tower even when we aren't seeking fish and even when the sea turns too rough—I reluctantly call them down and they reluctantly climb down, grasping the ladder, laughing, wet with spray.

In the predawn darkness the alarm buzzes, and I stumble into the bathroom. I see my face with its blotchy sun damage, the skin coarsened under the tan. I feel the tops of my ears, hardened and permanently numb. I think, briefly, of the extra precautions

I should be taking but know I won't—and the advice of one doctor to "limit your exposure time by staying out of the tower as much as possible"; I laugh at that one (the doc obviously had never been there). This life may kill me, but I'll be damned if I'll "limit my exposure" to it. There are few enough mornings in our lives, and on this one the rising sun will find me riding in the tower, bound offshore with the wind in my hair and my heart singing in joy.

• • •

There are three elements to catching a fish with a lure or with bait, and they are location, presentation, and attitude. Location means simply that you must be where there are fish at the right time to catch them. Actually doing it isn't so simple and involves a lifetime of studying fish behavior, aquatic biology, weather, coastal geology, tides and currents, and the structure of the water column. The learning never ends, which keeps fishing interesting, and I guess that an expert is just an old-timer with a good memory. Actually, that word makes me very nervous. "Expert" should only be applied to a skill, like tying knots or casting a fly rod, and never to a perpetually evolving process. To call oneself an expert fisherman is arrogant. And the fishing gods do not smile upon arrogance.

Presentation means creating an illusion that fools the fish into grabbing something with a hook in it. The illusion may be simple, such as a gob of clam on the bottom to represent a free lunch to a passing fish, or it may be complex, such as a spread of trolling lures to represent a school of panicky baitfish to a marlin or tuna, but the better the illusion, the more fish you catch. In fact, the gob of clam may not be so simple. Successful bait fishing, especially for wary species, requires attention to such elements as hook and leader visibility and judicious chumming—enough to attract fish and stimulate their feeding but not enough to make them stay down current, away from the boat, waiting for a free meal. As far as trolling is concerned, the choice, rigging, and placement of lures is an art, in which one bad or misplaced element can spoil the entire illusion.

The third part of catching a fish is attitude. Whether or not a fishing trip will be successful is often determined before the boat leaves the dock. If you aren't convinced that you will catch your fish, you probably won't. If you don't believe that you can win a tournament, you are doomed to lose. If you don't believe that you can catch a world-record fish, you won't. As simple as this idea seems, it is too little appreciated by most anglers.

Actually, that attitude counts shouldn't be all that surprising. One of the hottest topics in sports training these days is mental management, or what we used to call "attitude adjustment." There exist courses and books and videotapes and regimens all designed to apply the wonders of high technology to the same purpose as the old-time football pep rally. Modern athletes are well aware that developing and controlling their mental state is as important to winning as their physical training. And it shows. It is hard to think of a single sport where the best of yesteryear could seriously compete with the best of today.

"But," you say, "this isn't the Super Bowl! I go fishing for relaxation and enjoyment." Well, yes, but there is a basic paradox at work here. You may chase tuna, shark, or striped bass for relaxation and enjoyment, but fishing is an aggressive pursuit that attracts aggressive personalities. People who say that catching fish isn't what's important in fishing are wrong. Catching fish is what it's all about. A day when you don't catch fish may turn out to be a good day for any number of reasons, but if I tried to sell charters for "relaxation and enjoyment" I would be out of business in a very short time.

The worst example of bad attitude I ever experienced was when a five-man charter boarded the EARLY BIRD one morning for a tuna trip and one of the group said, "Look, I'd like to get back a little early this afternoon, 'cause both of us know this is just an expensive boat ride."

Surprised, I said, "What are you talking about?"

He replied, "We booked this trip in the spring, but I've been keeping up with what's going on, and they aren't getting any now."

As a matter of fact, the fishing hadn't been very good, but by working hard at it the better boats had been taking one or two tuna most days—and a few days after this exchange a large body of fish moved into range and it suddenly turned red hot. But at this moment it was me that turned red hot. "I don't know who *they* are," I said, "but *they* don't fish on *this* boat! *We* don't go out for expensive boat rides, *we* go out to find fish!"

My anger did no good. I went farther that day and stayed out longer than could possibly be profitable. But this man's attitude had poisoned the group. They were inattentive and spent the day napping and playing cards. They ignored weed checks of the trolling baits, and they were sloppy with the gear. We finally returned to the dock, skunked, although a number of yellowfin tuna were taken that day and one of my competitors had boated five. Our fishing effort had been thwarted by nothing more than bad attitude.

After years or research into the causes of sexual dysfunction in hundreds of people, Masters and Johnson concluded in their famous study that "the primary human sex organ is between the ears." I believe that their point applies to fishing as well; the primary piece of fishing gear is between the ears. More fishing trips, particularly offshore trips, are doomed by attitude than have ever been ruined by poor or faulty equipment. The difference between catching and not catching can be so subtle that it is subconscious—missing a weedline or a temperature break, or having a trolling lure not just right—the result of a small inattention that comes from a defeatist attitude.

The best example of the effect of a positive attitude I have ever seen was a customer I had several years ago who told me he was the luckiest man alive and one of the luckiest who had ever lived! Andy had been a paratrooper in World War II, had jumped into France on D-day, and had been one of the very few in his unit to survive intact. After the war he took a near-defunct company and made a fortune with it. He had an optimism about everything he did that bordered on the manic, and the concept of failure did not exist in his mind. When Andy was on the boat we always seemed to have a good day, whatever species we were after. Once he even took a 320-pound giant bluefin tuna on a codfish jigging rod with a VI-KE jig on 50-pound test line with no leader!

Andy was an excellent angler, but did he possess some magical aura of luck? Of course not! The plain fact is that his optimism was so infectious that everyone on the boat caught it. Everyone became more alert and subconsciously more attuned to the little things—the subtleties that separate the successful day of fishing from the "expensive boat ride." Knowledge and experience are both important, but Andy taught me that the very first and most vital requirement to becoming a successful offshore angler is a positive and optimistic attitude.

• • •

The expression "offshore fishing" or "offshore sport fishing" brings to mind blue water, leaping billfish, colorful thread wraps on custom fishing rods as thick as your thumb, gold-plated reels, heavy fighting chairs, polished teak, and the big, fast fishing yachts that smell of arrogance and too much money. A walk down one of the docks where these gleaming fiberglass "war wagons" tie up can be intimidating to those of more normal means. Even their hired crews seem aloof and more than a bit snooty. "Damn," you think, "how can I compete with this?"

The answer is, "Very well, indeed!" A war wagon may fish from Cape Cod to Costa Rica, but its crew will never be as familiar with a particular area as are the local fishermen. The sheer size of the vessel can even be a disadvantage. Tommy Gifford, the archetype of the offshore charter captain, became famous partly through his exploits in STORMY PETREL, his twenty-six-footer, and near the end of his life told George Reiger (in a conversation recorded in Reiger's fine book, *Profiles in Saltwater Angling*) that he considered a thirty-one-foot, diesel-powered, fiberglass boat to be the "ultra, ultra, ultra, ultra in big-game fishing boats." Tommy's last boat, CARIBE MAID, was a forty-two-footer, but he found her clumsy, saying, "You don't use a draft horse to play polo." One afternoon a few years ago, the owner of a sixty-three-foot war wagon looked wistfully at my EARLY BIRD, which nearly matches Tommy Gifford's ideal, and made me a tongue-in-cheek offer of an even trade. When I told him I thought his boat was beautiful and worth far more than mine, he replied that yes, it was, but he didn't have much fun with it. "It's a pain in the ass, dragging a damned condominium all over the ocean," he said.

The war wagons rarely came north of Montauk Point until about twenty-five years ago, so were not a part of New England's sport-fishing scene during its formative years. Also, in southern New England, far more than anywhere else, the very notion of what constitutes "offshore" fishing has evolved considerably, even during my lifetime. Our traditional big-game fish was the bluefin tuna, with an occasional swordfish or mako shark thrown in. Even our methods were defined by our local traditions. Giant bluefin, usually over four hundred pounds, were taken on bait while chumming within sight of the mainland, and school bluefin, usually under sixty pounds, were taken by trolling feathered jigs and cedar plugs within sight of Block Island. There was no need for blazing speed in those days, and the charterboats, many of which were based on commercial hulls, typically averaged from eight to eleven knots. Costs were low, and even by the standards of the time, the price of a charter was a bargain. The first sixteen-knot boat to enter the fleet was spoken of in reverential tones and described as a "rocket ship."

The decimation of the schools of small bluefin by purse seiners from the Pacific in the late sixties and early seventies upset this long-standing applecart. Yankee charterboats began to explore farther offshore, and higher speed became necessary to keep from eating up too much of the day in travel time. Nowadays, a sixteen-knot boat is ho-hum, and no one uses the term rocket ship any more. Before long we found ourselves way out of sight of land, in a domain that was already being fished by charterboats and war wagons from Montauk and points west. We soon discovered albacore tuna and learned new ways to fish. We learned that you don't have to troll for small tunas, but can chum them up and catch them on bait, just like we always had for the giants. We learned that you can catch giants by trolling, which pretty much completed the reversal of all we had known and done before. These techniques weren't new and shouldn't have been such a revelation to us, but you have to remember that Yankees have always tended to be parochial. We are also resourceful, and I remember one Yankee captain who bought a box full of children's jump ropes at a fire salvage sale, took the hollow handles with plastic tassels on their ends, strung leaders and hooks through them, and had super-cheap tuna lures—sort of the forerunners of today's expensive offshore trolling lures, and they worked just as well.

While we were moving farther offshore, yellowfin tuna were moving in from the Gulf Stream to meet us. No one knows why, but during those years the range of the yellowfin was extending farther north and onto the continental shelf south of New England and Long Island. As late as the early seventies, no landings of yellowfin had ever been recorded at Point Judith or any other Rhode Island port. The first ones were brought in around the mid-seventies, by the late seventies they had become common, and by the early eighties they had become established as our leading offshore fishery. But I have no confidence that they will stay in our waters. As I write, it is becoming necessary to go farther, year by year, to find yellowfin. The facts are that we never used to have them, we don't know why they suddenly appeared, and we certainly don't know how long they will continue to return. The older captains share my reservations and tend to look upon yellowfin tuna as no more than the fish that fortuitously came along and maybe, with luck, will pull us through the bluefin dearth. Our only future in offshore fishing may well lie not with the yellowfin, but with the hope of a restored bluefin fishery.

Our move offshore has been progressive but incremental—a bit more each year—until we now regularly fish waters that the old-timers would have thought impossible to reach in a single-day trip. Operating cost has escalated and with it the price of a charter. I heard one captain say that it seems to him that for every penny increase in the cost of fuel, the fish move a mile further offshore. What has happened, of course, is that all tuna stocks continue to be in decline, and it is necessary to go farther and look harder to find enough to make a good day.

The war wagons showed up in New England toward the end of the seventies, when the price paid for giant bluefin tuna shot up to obscene levels. But they had little impact here and have been pretty much gone since the decimation of the giants was completed. The new trend, not just in southern New England but on all the coasts, is toward the use of much smaller and faster boats to reach way offshore, fish for big-game species, and return to land, within a single day. The owners of these boats are affluent but not wealthy. Most are also articulate, and I admit that it is nice to have their numbers when it is time to fight for conservation of fisheries resources. Unfortunately, on the water they often lack the competence we grew used to when we dealt only with other charterboats and with war wagons operated by professional captains. These newly minted offshore anglers follow the well-known boats and often drive down fish by crossing chum lines and trolling too close. I recognize their right to be there, and I would not change the trajectory of our economic history, but it would be nice if people new to offshore waters and offshore fishing would learn the rules of the game before entering the arena.

• • •

The definitions of the words "ship" and "boat" are a bit vague, and there is really no distinct dividing line between them. Generally a ship is considered to be a large vessel designed to cross oceans and a boat is a smaller vessel designed for coastal use, although there is obvious overlap. I once read that a ship is a vessel large enough that it doesn't "roll, pitch, or yaw under conditions of normal sea state," although I have no idea what constitutes "normal sea state." I guess you could define it as whatever doesn't cause a ship to "roll, pitch, or yaw," which is a fine example of circular reasoning. You could also say that a boat is tethered to the coast and a ship is not.

Every boat has a maximum range that is dictated by size, design, fuel capacity, age, and state of repair, although it is all too common to see a boat pushed well beyond its legitimate range, sometimes by people who should know better. Ernest Hemingway once wrote, ". . . anyone who goes on the sea the year around in a small power boat does not seek danger. You may be absolutely sure that in a year you will have it without seeking, so you try always to avoid it all you can." Yet a well-known and popular fishing writer once told in print of his early days fishing the Northeast canyons at the edge of the continental shelf, nearly a hundred miles offshore, in a nineteen-foot outboard-powered open boat loaded with so many fuel drums that he couldn't stop the boat early in the trip or it would swamp. The tenor of the piece was along the lines of "what I did was dumb and *you* shouldn't try it," but the tone was clearly bragging. If he actually did what he described, he was both stupid and lucky to be alive. In the past decade I have experienced two bomb storms in which the sea went from calm to Beaufort sea state 7-plus, with breaking twelve-foot seas, in a matter of minutes. One was halfway to the canyons and the other was just off Block Island, and either would have flipped or swamped a nineteen-footer—in fact, the Block Island squall did flip a few boats of that size and swamped a twenty-four-footer.

Pushing a boat beyond its limits is by no means restricted to amateurs. Sebastian Junger's book, *The Perfect Storm*, and the movie based upon it tell the story of the loss of the F/V ANDREA GAIL with her entire crew during an unusually severe storm in the autumn of 1991. The captain and crew were all experienced high-seas fishermen and thoroughly competent seamen. Yet they were swordfishing on the Flemish Cap, nearly halfway across the North Atlantic Ocean, on a vessel that was originally designed for coastal commercial fishing on the continental shelf within a couple of hundred miles of shore. I fished one winter on a near-identical vessel (which was also later lost with all but one of its crew), and the thought of taking her to the Flemish Cap makes me shudder. The ANDREA GAIL had a steel hull, was seventy-two feet long, and had been set up for swordfish longlining with later modifications to increase her range. What couldn't be increased was the capacity of her internal fuel tanks, so to make it to nearly the middle of the ocean and back extra drums of fuel were strapped on deck. When I read this fact, I was reminded of the fishing writer with his nineteen-footer, and it struck me as equally stupid, though given the destruction of near-shore swordfish stocks, more understandable.

American boats are remarkably well made and seaworthy, if used as designed, but occasionally a marketing agency tries to oversell its product. Several years ago a twenty-five-foot, twin-outboard boat was featured in full-page ads in several national magazines as a "canyon special" that would routinely go to the edge of the continental shelf and be fishing in just two hours, implying an average speed of forty miles per hour; the ad quoted a "famous" Point Judith tuna captain to lend it legitimacy. I have fished from Point Judith for well over a quarter-century and have never heard of this "famous" captain, and when I asked around, no one else had heard of him either. The boat in question is, in fact, a superior product with excellent design and workmanship, but there are very few days when the sea would allow it to average forty miles per hour over such a distance. And, as any competent captain would agree, there is no twenty-five-foot boat made that belongs so far out into the North Atlantic Ocean, and it is criminally negligent to try to sell one for that purpose. I guess the company picked up on their overzealous marketing people, because the ad, thankfully, ran only a short time.

My EARLY BIRD is a bit over thirty-one feet long, diesel powered, with a down-east style hull that has a full keel and a skeg that protects the rudder and the propeller. She is rigged for tuna and considered sufficiently seaworthy to rate an insurance rider for a hundred miles offshore. I have fished the edge of the shelf with her a few times and have taken her as far as Veatch Canyon, which, although it is 122 nautical miles from Point Judith, is within my insurance limits since it is a bit over 80 nautical miles from Nantucket (a nautical mile, at 6080.2 feet, is longer than a land, or statute, mile, and equals one minute of latitude). But I consider a boat like EARLY BIRD to be the flat minimum for that kind of work and would prefer something larger if I were going to the edge and beyond on a regular basis. Nothing smaller, no matter how well designed or made, provides enough margin of safety when weather conditions unexpectedly turn bad or you are delayed by a breakdown. Going to Veatch is really pushing it.

There is a strange feeling I get—which others have similarly described—when I pass over the underwater cliff at the edge of the continental shelf in a small boat and my sounder shows the bottom quickly drop from a hundred to a thousand fathoms. It starts in my feet and works up, and soon I have the sensation of being suspended over a huge void, like the cartoon character who has run off a cliff but hasn't yet started to fall. Suddenly I know that I am truly alone and no longer connected to a continent. A cold thrill passes through me as I realize that there is an inch or so of fiberglass below my feet and then more than a mile to the bottom of the sea and that this is one place where I had better not screw up.

In *The Perfect Storm,* Junger's brilliant description of drowning is at the same time coldly clinical and intensely personal, and absolutely riveting. I read it before going to bed, and it left me sleepless and in a cold sweat; it should be read by anyone who intends to take any boat out of sight of land.

CHAPTER 11

Appleknockers and the First Northeaster;
Fishing for "Bees"; Haulout; Scientists and Politicians

The true biologist deals with life, with teeming boisterous life,
and learns something from it, learns that the first rule of life is
living.
—John Steinbeck, *The Log from the* Sea of Cortez, 1951

Ah, the great tragedy of science . . . a beautiful theory destroyed
by an ugly fact.
—Thomas H. Huxley, *Collected Essays,* 1893–94

The earth's atmosphere is a great, swirling storehouse of the
sun's energy, and sometime in late August or very early
September the sun's increasingly rapid movement toward
the equator produces an imbalance in that energy. The result for
the New England coast is the season's first northeaster.

This first winter-type storm forms in the boundary between two enormous air masses, one moist, tropical and oceanic,
the other dry, polar and continental. The strengthening, growing
mass of the polar air pushes against the weakening tropical air,
forcing it south and east from Canada toward the Atlantic along a
front that stretches for a thousand miles. When this cold front
reaches the coast and meets warm ocean water it stalls, forming a

line running all the way from Cape Hatteras to Nova Scotia. The denser, driving polar air knifes under the tropical air, wedging it upward and dropping its pressure, creating a storm of violently moving and spinning air in the zone of instability between the two colliding masses. The developing storm coalesces inside the southern part of the front, off Cape Hatteras, where the temperature and pressure gradients are steepest. Then it moves along the front, northward up the coast, releasing its pent-up energy as wild northeast wind and rain. The atmosphere's energy balance is restored, at least for a while, and summer returns for another month. But it isn't the same. There are no more hot nights, and the air seems, while not yet crisp, somehow brighter and drier. The harbingers of still greater impending changes begin to appear—a reddening leaf here, a line of swallows on a power line there—and the forests and fields are the deep green of old chlorophyll. Then, one day, you catch an appleknocker, and you know that the great migrations of autumn are beginning to stir.

Fishermen all over the world have their own names for the fishes they chase. In southern New England, little tunny, *Euthynnus alletteratus,* are called "appleknockers." I don't know what old salt first came up with that one, or even how long it has been used, but it must refer to the appearance of little tunny in our waters just as the apples are ripening, knocking on the door of the harvest time. Little tunny are more widely known along the East Coast as false albacore, a name I truly detest, since they are a distinct species that does not resemble the real albacore in any way other than sharing a few general tuna characteristics. Often the "false" is dropped, and they are referred to as "albacore," or "albies," leading to still further confusion.

Appleknockers are a true tuna, but their meat is very red, strong, and rather disagreeable. I have heard there is a way of cooking them that makes them palatable, but no one has ever told me what it is, and I cannot imagine eating one. Years ago, when school tuna fishing meant trolling feathered jigs and cedar plugs for small bluefin, they were considered something of a nuisance during the latter part of the season. But then along came a surge in saltwater fly fishing, and now appleknockers are all the rage.

In many ways appleknockers seem to have been designed to oblige the hordes of new fly fishermen. The fish move in close enough along the entire New England coast below Cape Cod to be readily available, even occasionally from shore, although it is a lot easier to follow them in a small, fast boat—I even see fly rodders in kayaks out there chasing them! They feed aggressively on small baitfish and take a streamer fly with no hesitation. They are mostly ten to twenty pounds, the world record being twenty-seven pounds, the perfect size for the same fly rod used on striped bass. Appleknockers are very strong and fight like all tuna, taking deep hard runs that make those little fly rods bend over double and those little fly reels scream for mercy. Finally, being virtually inedible, they don't present the politically correct fly rodder with a dilemma over killing a fish—most all of them are released.

The whole catch-and-release ethos caught me by surprise, and I still don't completely trust its sincerity. Is it a true movement, with depth and staying power, or simply another passing fad? Releasing fish is nothing new, and even when I was a boy there were outdoor writers touting it. In fact, Gifford Pinchot, a close friend of Teddy Roosevelt, wrote of catching and releasing fish a century ago. But releasing fish was always a minority perspective and usually seen as an option rather than some sort of moral commitment that renders the enlightened one superior to the coarse barbarian who would kill and eat a couple of fish.

I do find myself releasing a lot more fish these days than I ever used to, which must have my grandfather laughing in his grave. I can just hear that pragmatic old Yankee in his down-east accent, no hint of a smile but with a bit of a twinkle in his eye, saying, "What in'ell you want ta ketch a fish fer, if yer just gonna turn the sonofabitch loose?" My grandfather loved to fish, and I loved to go with him, but back then we would never have thought of releasing a fish. Nor would we catch more than we could use, although I don't remember being overly fastidious in our attention to legal limits. No matter how much time was consumed in preparations and travel, no matter how early we were on the lake or stream, when we got enough fish it was time to go home. Ten minutes or ten hours, the trip was over.

But my grandfather has been dead for almost forty years, and the world is so very much different from when I was a boy. The farmhouse burned down years ago and the land has been parceled and subdivided and the village up the road is a town and the town we visited once a month for supplies is now a city and the lake has vacation homes and hot bassboats and jet skis. Sometimes I am lonely for my grandfather and my heart bleeds for the way it was but can never be again, and I know that I must keep my memories locked away in a very special place because this new and different world can also be very good, but only if I learn to adapt. Maybe part of adapting is learning to release some of my fish.

If I am honest, I suppose my motives for releasing fish are less pure than the born-again catch-and-releaser. In the first place, I release nothing until I have enough for my own use (unless that would exceed the legal limit), and I enjoy eating most species of fish. When I first began fishing, this approach presented no real problem since I rarely caught enough to worry about wastage. As the years passed, my skills improved, and I began to catch more than I could use. But there was still no problem, since most of my fishing was in saltwater, and I could easily give away or sell the overage. More years passed; I worked on commercial fishing boats, worked on charterboats, owned my own charterboat—and I witnessed the decimation of almost every marine fishery. Something had to change for everyone, or there would be nothing left. For my part, I quit selling fish, and

I no longer allow my customers to sell them from the boat (although I can't control what they do after they leave). A charter-boat may be a commercial venture, but the customers are recreational fishermen, and the days of selling recreationally caught fish in the commercial marketplace are permanently behind us. Also, I hardly ever give away fish anymore. I guess I have become a crotchety old bastard, but I think of all the people I have given fish to over the years, and very few have ever reciprocated in any way. Let 'em go catch their own damn fish! Yet I can't see quitting and going home just because I have enough for myself. So now I just throw back the ones I can't use.

• • •

There are some times and there are some places when the ocean swarms with pulsing, teeming, vibrant life. Such a time and place is autumn in the inshore waters south of New England. New England's harvest time coincides with the two months between the arrival of the first large schools of appleknockers and the departure of the last large schools of striped bass. The hills and valleys turn bright with color, the corn is full eared and sweet, and roadside stands spring up on every country road with jugs of apple cider fresh from the presses, wagonloads of pumpkins and squashes, stacks of jars filled with homemade preserves, and pies still hot from hundreds of ovens. It is also harvest time for the sea creatures. From every estuary, salt pond, and cove, the ebb tides sweep out tons and tons of plant matter and algae and protozoans; and all across the bays, ledges, reefs, and sounds, billions of killifish and mummichogs and sand eels and bunker feed on this bounty and grow fat. They, in turn, fatten the great schools of predators—eating, eating, eating, in a frenzy of preparation for the grand migrations and the lean months of winter.

No matter how much I try to avoid doing so, during the harvest time I, too, add pounds of fat. It is not for lack of activity, because along with the gardening and the canning and the hunting, the fishing is the wildest and best of the entire year. After the sun passes the equinox, offshore runs for tuna rapidly taper off and the chilly mornings find us fishing inshore, chasing the four "bees"—bonito, bluefish, bass, and blackfish. Up and down the coast, school after school of bonito, bluefish, and bass, sometimes separate, sometimes mixed together, cover acres and acres of the surface—swirling, jumping, slashing—killing and eating all they can hold, gulls and terns screaming and diving into the slaughter, the water slick with fish oil and blood. Did I use the word "spectacular" yet? Cast into the melee with a spoon, a plug, or a fly, or troll its periphery, and one of the frenzied predators all but yank the rod out of your hand. If the school sounds, move on and you quickly find another, or stop and chum with ground bunker and chunks of bait and you can keep it going for most of the day. If the wind rises and the weather turns bad, you can find a rock pile in protected water somewhere to anchor on, put down a chumpot, and catch buckets of blackfish on crabs.

But for all the frenzied joy there is sadness as well. Part of this sadness may be the knowledge that the end is near and a long winter looms. I am a skier, and I love snowy slopes and hot soup and bright fireplaces, so why the sadness? The joy of autumn's sea harvest is genuine enough, but it is always tempered by the re-membrance of what has been lost, an understanding of the fragility of what is left, and a desire to save as much as we can for ourselves and those who follow. Fishing the "bees" is the year's crescendo, the final coda of a symphony both deep and complex, and its end is both sad and inspiring. We know that we have glimpsed into the soul of the Composer and felt the pulse of our own mortality.

• • •

For me, the fishing year always ends suddenly, like a door slamming shut in my face. I am knee-deep in fish, and then I wake up one day and it is over. The great migrations have taken the fish away, and the ocean looks gray and barren. All at once it is time to decommission the boat, haul it out, block it up, and make some sort of assessment of the year, both in the fishing logbook and the financial account book. I hope the logbook will reveal which fisheries are good enough to promote for next year's business and the account book will show enough income to satisfy the bank and carry us over the winter.

Decommissioning begins with stripping the boat. First, the truck is backed down to the head of the dock. Then it's into the marina restaurant for a cup of coffee and maybe a hotdog or a hamburger and a discussion with whoever is around of the state of the world, the venality of politics, or the lousy weather. Next, it's down to the boat where fishing gear and electronics are cleaned, packed, and removed to the truck, usually with one or more coffee breaks for further important discussions with whoever happens to walk down the dock.

Decommissioning for the winter never achieves the urgency felt at the beginning of the season. Sometimes it takes two or three days at a truckload per day, and as I pile up the shed I wonder how so much stuff managed to accumulate on the boat during the course of the year. I could probably gain a half-knot or more simply by winnowing out the useless gear, especially the latest, super-duper tuna lures that I figured I needed to have but never used. Sometimes during a coffee break I mention this phenomenon while pointing to a particular example and am informed that the lure or piece of gear in question actually *is* much better, but that I rigged it improperly and failed to bring out its best qualities. This, of course, ensures its place on the boat next year, and makes it certain that I will never realize that elusive additional half-knot.

Finally, all is done. My trip insurance has lapsed—I don't carry it during the high-premium "winter North Atlantic" months—and it is time to haul out. I fire up the diesel for the last time of the season, take off the dock lines, and slowly pull away from my slip and up the channel to the waiting haulout crew. For all the times I have made this short journey, the one thing I always remember is being struck by how low the December sun is in the sky, how long the shadows are, how muted the light is, even at midday.

I turn to port, pass a row of empty slips, center my rudder, shift to neutral, and then briefly reverse to stop the forward motion of the boat as it glides onto the slings; as they tighten on the hull I push the stop solenoid button and shut down the engine. The last thing I do as the boat is lifted from the water is climb the tower and take down the American flag from its halyard. The EARLY BIRD is now decommissioned for winter storage. There are still a few chores to finish, such as powerwashing the hull, draining the pumps and heat exchanger, and winterizing the head, but for me the end of the year is sharply defined by the lowering of the flag.

I have always flown the Stars and Stripes from a flag halyard high up on my boats—at least the ones large enough to have a flag halyard—for reasons both practical and symbolic. The flag's practical function is to serve as an inexpensive wind gauge, giving me at a glance a feel for the wind's speed and direction. This is important, but it is not really the *point* of it—any other flag or ensign or even a simple sailor's telltale would do the job. But I require that it be the Stars and Stripes. The Stars and Stripes will fly from the top of the halyard whenever EARLY BIRD is in commission and for as long as I am her captain.

Woodrow Wilson once said, "The flag is the embodiment, not of sentiment, but of history." I do not fly the Stars and Stripes high over EARLY BIRD to express "the postures of pretended patriotism" that George Washington, in his farewell address, warned against or any other superficial sentiment, but rather to place myself within the history of a civilization whose ideals are our only hope for the future. Sometimes I am depressed and angry with depleted fisheries resulting from nonsensical regulations. At such times, I look at the flag and know that the genesis of the problem lies in the eternal nature of the human animal. The founding fathers understood this nature and created a system that allows me to a part of its solutions. The flag reminds me that the fight is worth the effort.

• • •

Atlantic bluefin tuna are severely depleted and may, in fact, be approaching a population crash as a result of years of commercial overharvesting. Therefore, the primary goal of tuna management is supposed to be a recovery in their numbers. In light of the severity of the devastation, a total closure would be the best way to effect such a recovery, but such a move is neither politically nor economically feasible. Instead, we fish under a system of national quotas set each November by the representatives of the member nations of the International Commission for the Conservation of Atlantic Tunas (ICCAT) in Madrid, Spain. This entire quota system is based on hypocrisy, however, since ICCAT actually did close the bluefin fishery in 1982, but left a thinly-disguised loophole by allowing national quotas "for scientific monitoring purposes only."

The U.S. quota is administered and enforced by the National Marine Fisheries Service through a system of subquotas issued to each user group (purse seiners, harpooners, longliners, charterboat operators, recreational anglers, commercial rod-and-reelers) for each size classification and, in some cases, even for specific geographic areas. The bluefin tuna is valuable, and quotas are limited, so each winter the various user groups engage in "the winter follies"—a highly charged game of political football to try to gain a few more fish at the expense of one or more of the other groups. The requirements of proper scientific monitoring don't even enter into the discussions. In one of his *Conservation Watch* articles on bluefin tuna, Al Ristori described NMFS as a "failed agency." In an open letter to the Maine Coastal Conservation Association, George Reiger stated that he "despises" NMFS as "morally and scientifically bankrupt." These are strong words from two mature and widely read writers. Unfortunately, they ring true. NMFS, through its mismanagement of our nation's marine fisheries, has been consistent in only one thing—proving itself to be incapable of performing its assigned task.

Among the many records of NMFS failure, the tale of the Atlantic bluefin tuna is probably the worst and certainly the most bizarre. Carl Safina, fisheries authority and director of the Living Oceans Program, has called bluefin tuna "the most purposely mismanaged large animal in the world." Bluefin tuna management (and, to be fair, not just by NMFS but at higher levels of government both here and abroad) has been so outlandish and inconsistent that it has fueled widespread rumors of back-room deals and conspiracies, although I have found little hard evidence of such malfeasance. There *is* corruption in our National Marine Fisheries Service, but it is of a type that exists at the lowest levels of all mismanaged organizations and can best be described as ineptitude.

Yet we must try to understand what has gone wrong, or we will never repair the damage, and the bluefin tuna, along with the other great creatures of the oceans, will surely and finally disappear. Comparisons with the buffalo and the passenger pigeon have become trite but are nonetheless true. I tried to figure it all out when I came to write this section. I reviewed my files from four decades of bluefin laws and regulations; I reread my logbooks and personal notes; I read and talked with writers, fishermen, biologists, bureaucrats, conservationists, and politicians; I reflected—and still the picture isn't complete. I know the history, but I don't really *understand* it. I wanted to write it out here, step by step, so that others could see what happened and maybe help to avoid such things in the future, but the puzzle has too many missing pieces. All I can do is tell the small part of the story I have actually witnessed and hope that it gives the flavor of the whole.

Perhaps the greatest of NMFS sins has been the misuse of science and permitting the corruption of the people involved with gathering and interpreting data. By law, NMFS fisheries management is carried out through regulations based upon "the best available science," an expression that is one of those legislative details within which the devil is reputed to reside. By not specifying any performance standard other than a nebulous "best available," Congress ensured that the quality of the "best available" science would be low (which may have been the actual intent of those who framed the original legislation). Even science's tried-and-true quality-control system, outside peer review, was implicitly excluded.

To apply the word science to the farce that has resulted from this best-available requirement is euphemistic. Yet NMFS has managed to retain some semblance of scientific respectability for two reasons. First, NMFS science is not all bad. The service actually has some real scientists doing real, outside-peer-reviewed fisheries science, although their work has little direct impact on most politically sensitive fisheries management decisions.

Science is really nothing more than a way of learning the mechanical workings of the universe. It begins with measured observation and proceeds to forming hypotheses and gathering facts (often by experiments, which are nothing more than comparisons between what is known and what is not). The separate facts are then put together into theories that try to explain how things work (the inductive reasoning part). A theory that can be used to predict future events is called a scientific law. And that really is all there is to it—no matter how many big words or how much obfuscation is thrown into it.

In *Symbiotic Planet,* renowned biologist Lynn Margulis said that "one must always strive to distinguish bullshit from authenticity." Nobel prize winner Konrad Lorenz wrote in *King*

Solomon's Ring, "Every scientist should, after all, regard it as his duty to tell the public, in a generally intelligible way, about what he is doing." He also defined "specious cover for ignorance of fact" as "contemptible dilettantism." NMFS has had too many such dilettantes. I call them "science bullshitters" to reflect their lack of loyalty to the ideals of true science and their willingness to sell out to political expediency. In his recent book, *The Striped Bass Chronicles,* George Reiger takes a less severe view, calling them "biocrats" who "seem more concerned with forms, procedures, and maintaining control than with achieving goals." Either way, NMFS has based too many tuna management decisions on their flawed pronouncements.

My first encounter with an NMFS "biocrat" was a revelation. It was during a winter hearing on bluefin tuna allocations for the following season, which was being held at NMFS headquarters in Silver Spring, Maryland. The official had completed a review of the catch data for the year just past—data that would be used to determine our next-year quota. It was well known in the industry that the data from the angling category was soft. He had presented it in precise numbers, so I raised my hand and asked if he had any feel for the reliability of the data. His quick answer that the data was "totally reliable" drew a murmur from several charter captains and caught me by surprise. I rephrased the question: "What are your confidence limits for that particular statistic?" I asked. His eyes narrowed, but his voice was strong as he replied, "Ninety-five percent!"

I felt my blood rising. "The raw data is far too imprecise to support that confidence level," I said.

"We have other data sources and use several statistical tests," he replied.

"Which ones?" I asked.

"We use several *very* precise statistical models, but they are *quite* complicated," he said. This was the exact moment of my epiphany. I suddenly saw, with total clarity, the sham that is the foundation of tuna management. For the first time in my life I was actually face-to-face with a real-life science bullshitter.

"I would like to see the data sets and the models that you use," I said.

He stared at me for a long moment. Then he looked down at the table in front of him and said, "Certainly. I have that information right here." He shuffled some papers and said, "It will take me a few moments to put my hands on it. Meanwhile, let me take another question." He pointed to someone else and, in a neat move, slipped away. A while later, someone in the audience pointed to me and yelled, "Hey, you didn't answer this guy's question!" But it was too late.

Later, I found myself in the elevator alone with one of the three U.S. representatives to ICCAT. Looking straight ahead, he said, "You were right. The data isn't any good. They won't admit it, and neither will I, but in private sessions the Japanese ridicule our numbers." He neither looked at me nor said anything else. The elevator stopped at the ground floor, we both walked away, and I knew that I had been playing in a game where I didn't even know the rules.

Science begins with observation, normally measured or quantified, that is recorded as what we loosely call data. The Latin word *data* used to be reserved strictly for the results of formal experiments, but the advent of computers has broadened the meaning to also include the record of any observation. To any reasonable person, no scientific conclusion can be any better than the quality of the recorded data that supports it, yet NMFS has continued to make decisions on the management of truly important fisheries resources based upon data that is known to be flawed and in some cases fraudulent.

In order to maintain a quota system for the harvest of any natural resource, be it bluefin tuna, ducks, deer, or trees, it is necessary to know how many are taken. You must either directly count them or accurately estimate their numbers. Tuna that are caught and sold can be tagged and counted at the point of sale. But anglers keep their fish, and there are thousands of them at hundreds of ports, so a direct count is more difficult, and NMFS uses statistical estimates. To be accurate, such estimates must use statistical models that include size and both spatial and temporal distribution of the fleet, average time engaged in fishing, and average number of fish taken. These numbers are determined by taking random samples, which are simply recorded observations or, in a word, data.

NMFS does not have sufficient personnel to gather all the catch data from all the anglers in all the ports, so it contracts this work out to a private company. The first bluefin tuna contractor, a company called KCA Research, hired part-timers at minimum wage and with no training sent them out to do dockside polling of fishermen and to count fish. Most of these "data gatherers" didn't know a tuna from a tugboat, and none of them could distinguish a bluefin from a yellowfin tuna. Yet the form they originally used had entries for twenty-five different species, using common names that aren't the same from one end of the coast to the other. Many fishermen had great fun playing with the data gatherers, and the data they gathered was mostly wrong. Then things got much worse and still later downright ugly.

One day, during the latter part of the 1992 tuna season, Al Conti stopped me as I was walking up the dock. Al owns Snug Harbor Marina, where I tie up; his office sits at the head of the main dock and has a large window overlooking the whole operation. "Dave," he said, "there's something funny going on with these data collecting people."

"Really? I haven't seen them around much this year," I said.

"Yeah, well, they've been around most every day," he said. "They show up two or three hours after you guys all leave, and they're long gone by the time you get back in. I see them from my window, reading the paper and drinking coffee at the picnic table. Sometimes I see them writing on their clipboards."

"You suppose they're turning in phony reports?" I said.

"Hell, yes!" Al's voice was raised. "And I'll bet they are getting paid for all the time they're not here!"

This sort of petty corruption is so common that I sort of laughed it off at the time, particularly since the data takers had proven so incompetent when they actually tried to do their job. But as I thought about it I wondered just what they *were* reporting. Then, like a shot out of nowhere, NMFS announced that the angling quota was filled and would be closed from September 23 to the end of the calendar year. Although we all knew that only a fraction of the quota could possibly have been taken, every Montauk and New England charterboat was suddenly put out of business for the last month of the bluefin season, causing large economic losses not only to the fleet but to local motels, fuel and bait dealers, marinas, tackle shops, and restaurants. Now I *really* wanted to know what was in those reports!

But it wasn't easy to find out. Both the research company and NMFS refused to provide me with copies of the data sheets for my boat, nor would either tell me what was reported on them. I called Capt. Joe McBride, Chairman of the Montauk Boatmen and Captains Association, and Steve Sloan, trustee of the International Game Fish Association, and through political pressure and the threat of a lawsuit NMFS finally relented. On January 21, 1993, they hastily put together a written "Policy for Data Requests of NMFS Large Pelagic Survey Program Interview Forms" and agreed to meet with us later in the spring to turn over the copies.

The meeting was held in the Challenger Room at the Pell Marine Science Library in Narragansett, Rhode Island. This location struck me as ironic, since its namesake, Senator Claiborne Pell, a man for whom I have unbounded admiration, did so much during his career to advance real science. There were seventeen people at the meeting, including the head of KCA Research and his Rhode Island representative, and eight NMFS officials, including the chief of the Highly Migratory Species Management Division. They had rolled out the big guns, although all seemed a bit nervous. Steve Sloan was there, as well as Al Conti, Joe McBride, and four other charterboat captains from New York, Connecticut, and Rhode Island. One of the NMFS people was Dr. Jack Casey, whom I had asked to attend because he is an old friend, a widely respected scientist, and one of the world's leading experts on pelagic fish.

NMFS began the meeting with a presentation on data analysis that was elementary in nature and condescending in tone. When the official got to the part on estimating fleet size, I asked him what statistical method he used. "Oh," he answered, "We have a method called the mark and recapture model. I *could* explain it to you, but the math *is* rather complicated."

I had come to the meeting anticipating phony data, but here was a new problem. I guess the biocrat must have interpreted my stunned look as dumb acquiescence because he began to go on. *"Wait!"* I shouted. "I can't *believe* what I'm *hearing!"* I had used the mark and recapture method years before in my master's research. "The mark and recapture method *depends* upon a random chance of recapture, and the math is simple *ratios!* The model is totally inappropriate to your application! Your fleet size estimate has to be *way* off!" I turned to Jack Casey. "Jack, am I right on this?"

Jack leaned forward and frowned. "You're exactly right," he said. "Mark and recapture doesn't work the way they're using it."

This guy was smooth. He only hesitated a moment before saying, "We have confidence in our statistics," then he started off in a new direction.

But he didn't get very far. Steve Sloan slammed his hand down on the table and shouted, *"Enough* of this! We didn't *come* here to listen to *bullshit! We came* here to get *raw data sheets!* Turn them over *now* or we walk and you'll turn them over in front of reporters in a courtroom!"

Nobody moved or said anything. Steve stood up and began to gather his papers, and the rest of us followed suit. The head of KCA Research said, "I have the data sheets right here. We just thought you might like to . . ."

"Then turn them over *right now*," Steve interrupted.

"Yes, they are right here, you can look them over and get back to us." He stood up and began to turn toward the door.

"Not so fast," Steve said. "These captains brought their logbooks. Let's compare notes *right now!*"

The man turned back to the table, and I could see that his face had paled and his hands shook a bit. And with good reason, as it turned out. Much of the catch data supposedly taken from my boat was phony, the sheets pure fabrication. One in particular could even be independently corroborated: the data sheet had me fishing fifty miles offshore and catching five bluefin tuna, even giving their lengths and weights; but I had taken out a local attorney that day with a group of his clients to fish for striped bass and bluefish close to shore and then I took them to Block Island for lunch. The attorney was even willing to give a deposition to that effect. KCA Research was trapped, and they knew it. NMFS didn't look so hot, either, although they seemed to be shocked by it all.

By the time we left the meeting, KCA had agreed to fire everyone involved and to allow the state charterboat associations to help train their personnel. They may have lived up to the first, but they never lived up to the second. NMFS pretty much washed their hands off the whole incident, although they didn't renew their contract with KCA. The big losers were the businesses that suffered the effects of an early quota shutdown brought on by fraudulent data, showing fish that were never caught.

By the beginning of the 1993 tuna season, the situation had become very tense. Fishermen began refusing to speak to anyone from NMFS or from their contractors, and in Rhode Island there were several ugly incidents. Marina operators ordered data takers off their property, invoking trespass laws. After Al Conti denied them access, he was visited by a NMFS enforcement officer, who told him that he was required by federal regulation to allow agents of NMFS or any of its contractors onto his property to conduct their surveys. Al was furious. In addition to the business he had lost during the early closure, he had been stuck with thousands of pounds of tuna bait that he had paid for but couldn't sell. "Why should I allow anyone onto my property who puts me out of business with *lies?*" The agent responded by threatening him with arrest if he failed to comply.

Throughout the 1993 season, I refused data takers access to my boat or my customers, although I knew this was a clear violation of fisheries regulations. I simply didn't trust either their competence or their honesty. At one of the hearings during the following winter, I was approached by an NMFS official whom I knew. He said, "What the hell's going on in Rhode Island? It's like you guys are starting a revolution up there. Our data takers are afraid to even go on the docks!"

"Why are you surprised?" I asked. "How do you think revolutions get started? You people fucked us over, then hid behind stupid regulations, and now you're surprised that we're pissed off?"

He gave me the expected platitudes about how they were trying to do better and how we all had to work together, and I told him that I agreed about the working together part, but things had become so polarized that I didn't see how, and that was how we left it.

By 1994, every bluefin tuna user group was fed up with NMFS. On the other side, there were powerful conservation organizations calling for an end to all commercial trade in bluefin under the Endangered Species Act. The pressures were building, and in our open political system such things can go just so far before checks and balances kick in. In early 1994 it finally happened. Under intense political pressure from all sides, NMFS was forced to ask the National Research Council for "independent advice on the scientific basis of management for Atlantic bluefin tuna." It was very late in the game, but finally there would be an outside peer review by people who really knew their business.

The NRC is the operating arm of the National Academy of Sciences (NAS), which is a private, nonprofit society of the most distinguished scientists in the country. The NAS received a congressional charter in 1863, during the Lincoln administration, "to advise the federal government on scientific and technical matters." New members are voted in by their peers based solely on their record of scientific accomplishment. This process has made the academy a nonpolitical "council of elders" and a longstanding national resource of immeasurable value.

The 148-page NRC review, *An Assessment of Atlantic Bluefin Tuna,* was completed, published, and distributed before the November 1994 ICCAT meeting, an amazing accomplishment for such a short time. It was a masterpiece that surpassed everyone's expectations for thoroughness and logic, and it injected scientific rigor into the management debate. Without pointing fingers or seeking blame, its cool, dispassionate tone was like a dash of cold water that suddenly awoke the warring factions to how stupid and counterproductive we had all become. The report didn't pretend to have all the answers, but it sure told us what we had to do.

Among its many recommendations, two are of importance to that small part of the tuna battles to which I had been a party. Under "Quality Control," the report states, "The first link in the chain of quality control is data collection. . . . Samplers should be carefully supervised and evaluated." At its very end, the report criticizes prior research and concludes with perhaps its most important recommendation, "The committee recommends that review of all research proposals and resulting manuscripts include a process of external peer review."

In the years since the NRC report, NMFS has improved its performance on American quota allocations, although it may be too late for a significant recovery of the bluefin tuna, at least in my lifetime. International issues remain unresolved, and the agency's ability to affect the outcome has been curtailed. The worst legacy of the biocrats has been the continued hostility toward science. Fishermen who should have been part of the solution are now part of the problem. Catches of bluefin tuna are reported that don't occur, and many catches that do occur are never reported, all in order to skew the numbers for some perceived personal advantage. For many, the attitude has become, "Hell, the scientists don't know what's going on, so grab all you can."

Understandable though this attitude may be, the fact remains that the only hope for saving the last of one of the ocean's most magnificent creatures is in learning more about them—in other words, in good science. In an interview for the journal *Nature*, Terrance J. Quinn, a member of the NRC panel, said, "It is almost appalling that the basic data needed for managing the population is not there." Speaking of NMFS in the same piece, John J. Magnuson, the chairman of the panel, said, "They have to use the best available science. We need better data—but its absence can't be used as an excuse not to use what we have." I would add that I hope that the work of the NRC panel makes it so that the requirement to use "the best available science" will no longer be used as an excuse for poor work.

Although there has been great improvement in their application, NMFS continues to use statistical modeling to manage the angling quota for bluefin tuna, to open and close seasons and change bag limits on too short notice, and this policy continues to unnecessarily harm businesses that require long-range planning and continuity. Charterboats and motels book customers as long as a year in advance, and marinas must contract for bait and fuel weeks before it is needed. Not knowing what you have to work with from day to day is expensive and frustrating. NMFS has made a good-faith effort to mitigate the harm, especially since the late nineties, but a whole new approach is needed. An appropriate model might be the successful management of deer herds with fixed, predetermined seasons and required tags.

Bluefin tuna range throughout the world's tropical and temperate oceans, so my experience with their worldwide management is limited and, perhaps, parochial, as any single fisherman's must be. The problems in the bluefin tuna fisheries, as well as those in all other fisheries, are larger and far more complex than any single book can encompass. But their importance cannot be overemphasized. The fate of the human species is entwined with the fate of the fishes of the sea in ways that we still do not completely understand.

One of the most enduring criticisms of fisheries management is that it is "too political." I have no patience with that argument. Politics is how the world works. The system may be messy and it may be slow, sometimes agonizingly so, but it only really breaks down when citizens become apathetic and don't fight for their interests. I have found that a persistent and well-informed individual can be surprisingly effective. Venality, corruption, and greed are always players in the process, and we must accept these darker "angels of our nature" for what they are—enemies of human progress. If we aren't willing to work to make the pie bigger and fight for our piece of it, then we shouldn't whine when we find ourselves cut out and our lives impoverished. As for me, I'll be too busy to listen to such foolishness.

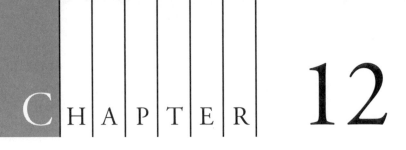

CHAPTER 12

The Sea; Charlatans; Changes; A Good World

They that go down to the sea in ships, that do business in
great waters, these see the works of the Lord, and his wonders
in the deep.
—Psalm 107:23–24

The call of the sea is a theme that has been a staple in literature at least since the time of Homer. And the idea of
there being some sort of mystic, magnetic force emanating
from the sea to the human spirit goes back further, back to a time
before writing, when people gathered around a fire and told stories
of the sea from which came legends of storms and strife, strange
creatures and monsters, terror and heroism.

The sea has always provided so many basic physical
needs. Food and salt are obvious ones, but even the ancients
knew that proximity to the sea moderated climate and was just
plain healthy. A boatbuilder and lobsterman on Beal's Island,
Maine, once said to me, "We don't make too much money up
here, but we're healthy, and as long as the tide keeps comin' in
and goin' out, I guess we'll eat good." We were seated at his table
eating steamed clams, lobsters, and finnan haddie made with
dried salt cod from his boat and potatoes and corn from his garden. His family had been on Beal's Island for generations, his

sons worked on the clam flats after school and dreamed of working on trawlers or shrimp boats or of some day owning their own lobster boats.

But there has always been an attraction to the sea that transcends food and reaches to a higher Providence. In *Moby Dick* Melville begins his tale with a description of this larger appeal in the very first paragraph:

> Call me Ishmael. Some years ago—never mind how long precisely—having little or no money in my purse, and nothing to interest me on shore, I thought I would sail about a little and see the watery part of the world. It is a way I have of driving off the spleen, and regulating the circulation. Whenever I find myself growing grim about the mouth; whenever it is a damp, drizzly November in my soul; whenever I find myself involuntarily pausing before coffin warehouses, and bringing up the rear of every funeral I meet; and especially whenever my hypos get such an upper hand of me, that it requires a strong moral principle to prevent me from deliberately stepping into the street, and methodically knocking people's hats off—then, I account it high time to get to sea as soon as I can. This is my substitute for pistol and ball. With a philosophical flourish Cato throws himself upon his sword; I quietly take to the ship. There is nothing surprising in this. If they but knew it, almost all men in their degree, some time or other, cherish very nearly the same feelings toward the ocean with me.

He then alludes to the higher Providence a bit later:

> ... Why is almost every robust healthy boy with a robust healthy soul in him, at some time or other crazy to go to sea? Why upon your first voyage as a passenger did you yourself feel such a mystical vibration, when first told that you and your ship were now out of sight of land? Why did the old

Persians hold the sea holy? Why did the Greeks give it a separate deity, and own brother of Jove? Surely all this is not without meaning. And still deeper the meaning of that story of
Narcissus, who because he could not grasp the tormenting,
mild image he saw in the fountain, plunged into it and was
drowned. But that same image, we ourselves see in all rivers
and oceans. It is the image of the ungraspable phantom of life;
and this is the key to it all.

This "ungraspable phantom of life" was on the mind of the
Preacher when he said, in the Book of Ecclesiastes (1:7), "All the
rivers run into the sea, yet the sea is not full; unto the place whither
the rivers go, thither they go again."

Implicit in these passages is the *return* of all things to the
sea in grand, recurring cycles, an ancient idea that modern biologists and earth scientists like to think they invented. The idea of
the sea as the mother of all life is more recent, but still more than
a century old. In *Twenty Thousand Leagues under the Sea*, Jules
Verne has Captain Nemo enthusiastically answer Professor Aron-
nax's question, "You love the sea, don't you, Captain?"

Yes, I love it! The sea is everything. It covers seven-tenths of the
globe. Its breath is pure and healthy. It is an immense desert
where a man is never alone, for he can feel life quivering all
about him. The sea is only a receptacle for all the prodigious, supernatural things that exist inside it; it is only movement and
love; it is the living infinite, as one of your poets has said. And
in fact, Professor, it contains the three kingdoms of nature—
mineral, vegetable, and animal. This last is well represented by
the four groups of zoophytes, by the three classes of articulata,
by the five classes of mollusks, by those innumerable legions of
fish, that infinite order of animals which includes more than
thirteen thousand species, only one-tenth of which live in fresh
water. The sea is a vast reservoir of nature. The world, so to

speak, began with the sea, and who knows but that it will also end in the sea!

This concept of a mystic, nurturing sea to which man magnetically returns contrasts with an even older tradition of the sea as siren, a place to which man is drawn and held, sometimes trapped, by forces, often supernatural, that are beyond his control. In the oldest Greek mythology, from a thousand years before Christ, the sea is ruled by the god Poseidon. Poseidon is a major god, brother both to Zeus, who rules man and all other gods, and Hades, who rules the earth and the underworld. He is a cruel and jealous god, sometimes violent and always unpredictable. Piqued by Laomedon, the king of Troy, Poseidon sided with the Greeks in the Trojan War. After the war he became hostile to Odysseus (Ulysses), one of the Greek leaders and ruler of the island of Ithaca, when Odysseus blinded Polyphemus, the Cyclops who was his son. He tormented Odysseus for ten years, preventing his ship from returning home and subjecting him to great tribulations. Even mighty Zeus would not intervene, although Odysseus had great favor in his eyes. In the opening scene of Homer's *The Odyssey*, the goddess Athena, distressed by his treatment, asks Zeus, "Did not Odysseus pay you honor by the Argive ships and offer sacrifices on the plain of Troy? Why then are you so wroth against him, Zeus?" His answer describes the power of the sea in the minds of the ancients:

> My child, what word has passed the barrier of your teeth? How could I possibly forget princely Odysseus, who is beyond all mortal men in wisdom, beyond them too in giving honor to the immortal gods, who hold the open sky? Nay, but Poseidon, the girdler of the earth, is ceaselessly enraged because Odysseus blinded of his eye the Cyclops, godlike Polyphemus, who of all Cyclops has the greatest power. A nymph, Thoosa, bore him, daughter of Phorcys, lord of the barren sea, for she within the

hollow caves united with Poseidon. And since that day earth-shaking Poseidon does not indeed destroy Odysseus, but ever drives him wandering from his land.

In Book XIII, Zeus, speaking directly to Poseidon, even more strongly affirms the power of the sea god:

> The gods do not refuse you honor. Hard would it be to cast dishonor on our oldest and our best. And as to men, if any, led by pride and power, dishonors you, vengeance is yours and shall be ever.

The most famous example in western culture of the control of the sea by a supernatural deity and its use in entrapping and punishing man is the story of Jonah. When Jonah attempted to flee God on a ship (Jonah 1:4), "Jehovah sent out a great wind upon the sea, and there was a mighty tempest on the sea, so that the ship was like to be broken." The other men on the ship threw Jonah over the side to appease God, who then "prepared a great fish to swallow up Jonah" (1:17). In the belly of the fish Jonah finally submits to God and the sea and offers up a prayer that brings about his salvation and includes these lines (2:3–5):

> For thou didst cast me into the depth, in the heart of the seas,
> And the flood was round about me;
> All thy waves and thy billows passed over me.
> And I said, I am cast out from before thine eyes;
> Yet I will look again toward thy holy temple.
> The waters compassed me about, even to the soul;
> The deep was round about me

From the ancients to the Bible to the Norse sagas to Columbus to the Flying Dutchman to sea serpents to *The Rime of the Ancient*

Mariner to the wreck of the PALATINE to Peter Benchley's *Jaws*, this theme of man against the sea with a strong dollop of the supernatural thrown in has remained a staple of our culture.

But in addition to the nurturing sea and the cruel sea there is yet a third major theme. The sea is also a liberator, a source of not just freedom but independence. Captain Nemo says:

> The sea does not belong to tyrants. On its surface, they can still exercise their iniquitous rights, fighting, destroying one another and indulging in other earthly horrors. But thirty feet below its surface their power ceases, their influence dies out and their domination disappears! Ah, Monsieur, one must live—live within the ocean! Only there can one be independent! Only there do I have no master! There I am free!

From the time of the Pilgrims, it has been the act of crossing the sea to the New World, breaking the chains of the past, that has imparted to Americans their belief in freedom as an essential guiding principle and their sense of their country as unique and, right or wrong, the world's last, best hope. How strange and contradictory that our greatest national shame—which led to our deepest and most persistent national schism—arose from the bitter act of forcing a people to cross the eternal sea in chains and against their will.

• • •

The sea does not suffer fools lightly. In fact, it can be pretty rough on liars. You can misrepresent yourself to other people and grow wealthy or get elected to high public office. But if you lie to the sea it destroys you and may even take your life. Examples abound: a drunken tanker captain who runs aground, a tug captain who loses a barge in a sea he knows to be too stormy, a yachtsman rammed in the fog because he failed to learn correct radio procedure; a fisherman who capsizes because his vessel is top heavy; an entire regional fishing industry destroyed and many of its people financially ruined because of their own delusions and the corruption of their leaders. These incidents are similar in the severity of their consequences. Drunks, fools, incompetents, and charlatans sometimes do well and even flourish on land. They never flourish and rarely survive at sea.

I think that I understand Ishmael. He was saying that his soul was equipped with a bullshit filter and that too-long association with landsmen clogged it up. Going to sea cleaned it out and made it possible for him to remain sane, or at least in possession of his soul. His filter may have been too finely wrought and easily clogged, perhaps to the point of some recognized pathology, but this cycle has become a part of my life as well. Toward the end of each winter I "find myself growing grim about the mouth," and I know that it is "high time to get to sea as soon as I can."

And it works. Twelve- to fourteen-hour days reduce my weight, my blood pressure, my cholesterol and sharpen my muscle tone, my senses, and my attitude. But mostly the changes derive from the old knowledge that I can't fool the sea and from something akin to Ishmael's "mystical vibration" at being "out of sight of land" and his image of the "ungraspable phantom of life" that go to work on me and clean out my filter and make it possible for me to survive in a world that sometimes seems filled with self-deluding fabricators. I can once again work with the honest and the real, ignore the charlatans, and most importantly clearly discern the differences and assign them their proper value. I know that other activities, such as a vacation in the mountains or engaging in vigorous sports, can have the same effect, but nothing seems to do it so well as time spent upon the ocean.

• • •

Twenty-two centuries ago, the Romans named the first month of the year after their god Janus, who presided over new beginnings. But Janus had two faces, one on the front of his head, looking forward, and the other on the back of his head, looking at what has just been. New beginnings are like that. So at the beginning of each new year I find myself not just looking ahead, into the future, but also reflecting upon the past. A decade ago, my comparisons were disheartening, at least as far as the future of the oceans and their living ecosystems was concerned. But it turns out that I am not much of a prophet. The sky didn't fall; there have been some new beginnings that I, unlike Janus, didn't foresee; and now, at the beginning of a new millennium, I see much less reason for pessimism.

Not that there isn't major damage to ocean ecosystems, and not that there won't be some difficult times ahead. But a fundamental change is occurring in our culture that bodes well for the future not just of our ocean fisheries but of all of our natural resources. There is a new ethic emerging, and although still nascent, it appears unstoppable because it is a natural evolutionary step from our traditional ethics and is based upon a new understanding of the nature of the universe and of our place in it.

More than a half-century ago, philosopher-conservationist Aldo Leopold identified three historical steps in the development of ethics. In his essay "The Land Ethic," he stated:

> The first ethics dealt with the relation between individuals; the Mosaic Decalogue is an example. Later accretions dealt with the relation between the individual and society. The Golden Rule tries to integrate the individual to society; democracy to integrate social organization to the individual.
>
> There is as yet no ethic dealing with man's relation to land and to the animals and plants which grow upon it. . . .
>
> The extension of ethics to this third element in human environment is, if I read the evidence correctly, an evolutionary possibility and an ecological necessity. It is the third step in a sequence. The first two have been already taken.

It is Aldo Leopold's proposed "third step" ethic that is now, finally, emerging. We must make certain that it becomes a reality, not only in our relationship to the land, but to the sea as well. Our increased ability to alter ocean ecosystems dictates this necessity. With no ethical compass we bumble, without direction, from crisis to crisis, pointing fingers at our favorite scapegoats, denying personal culpability, no more than impotent bystanders to the loss of our most precious assets.

The destruction of our fisheries took an amazingly short period of time—two decades for the groundfisheries, a decade for the pelagics. When my father was a commercial fisherman there were no depleted stocks, despite centuries of human harvest. When I bought my first charterboat we were still able to fish on more than three dozen species. A decade later, my business was carried by but a half-dozen species, the loss of any of which would have probably put me out of business. Now, after another decade, we are up to ten or so viable fisheries—a long way from being out of the woods, but at least we are going in the right direction.

Who do we blame for the destruction? The draggermen and gillnetters who destroyed the groundfishery, the longliners who destroyed the white marlin and swordfishery, the purse seiners who destroyed the bluefin tuna fishery, the charterboat captains who abused the pollock fishery and destroyed the bluefishery— none of them were evil people. They were generally ethical in their dealings with one another and with their society, yet there was clearly an ethical void in their conduct on the ocean. Their predicament and its result remind me of Lincoln's words in his Second Inaugural Address, delivered in the last weeks of the Civil War, a cataclysm resulting from another ethical void: "On the occasion corresponding to this four years ago, all thoughts were anxiously directed to an impending civil war. All dreaded it—all sought to avert it. And the war came." None of the fishermen intended to destroy the fisheries; all dreaded it—all sought to avert it. And the destruction came. Such a thing must never happen again, and fortunately, we can keep it from happening again as long as we complete Leopold's third step by extending ethics to our relationship to the sea, to the land, to our sustaining planet and its resources.

Where do we start? How do we codify a third-step ethic? All ethics are based upon shared assumptions, and a resource ethic must be based upon shared assumptions about humans and about the earth. Recently I co-authored a paper with Carl Safina based upon presentations we made at a Yale University conference in May 2000 on just this topic. Carl is the author of *Song for the Blue Ocean*, which is, very simply, the best book ever written on the plight of the world's fisheries and its implications for people everywhere. In our paper, "A Rising Tide for Ethics," we proposed the following six assumptions as a starting point:

1. The known universe was created at a specific time, has since then been changing, and will run a course.

2. The natural world is palpable to reason. It operates under natural laws that are knowable and consistent and which we are part of.

3. All living things alter their environment (for example, the current high level of molecular oxygen in the atmosphere was caused by photosynthetic organisms), and there is nothing inherently evil in this simple fact.

4. Humans have free will, even within the Creator's plan, and are the only organisms able to make conscious decisions to alter their environment. We do not possess the power to end life on the planet, but could end our own tenure.

5. Humans have an esthetic sense and a need to fulfill it. As Edward O. Wilson said in *The Diversity of Life*, "An enduring environmental ethic will aim to preserve not only the health and freedom of our species, but access to the world in which the human spirit was born."

6. All living things, humans included, act in their own perceived self-interest (the basis of natural selection).

These assumptions are based upon two very different points of view, one derived from faith and the other from reason. Until recently, to have considered them together in this fashion would have been philosophically absurd and practically impossible and would have seemed patronizing by each toward the other. After all, faith and reason have been sharply separated in western culture since the days of Roger Bacon in the late thirteenth century. The separation of the two, originally intended to strengthen faith, paradoxically allowed the rise of modern science and the secularization of modern society. But then a funny thing happened. As science probed the boundaries of the universe and of time and the basic structures of matter and of life, the two world views began to appear less incompatible. And now, in our time, they are beginning to be rejoined. Suddenly there is a profusion of books and articles and conferences on the new synthesis of those old antagonists, and the world now seems ready to accept that faith and reason are, and must always be, complementary forces in our lives. Both are needed to build an ethical foundation sufficient to support a continuing, self-sustaining civilization. Understanding this relationship can provide us a foundation upon which to build an ethic—a moral compass—for our relationship to our sustaining planet.

Our proposed six assumptions, taken together, appear to bear an internal conflict. They can be seen to justify behavior ranging all the way from purely altruistic to totally selfish. But this conflict resolves itself when we realize that altruism and self-interest lie at the two poles of our moral compass, apparently opposite but in fact conjoined. An ethical decision is guided by elements of both.

The problem from a scientist's standpoint is that altruism is difficult to justify on the basis of reason unless there is some larger purpose. But we can glimpse a larger purpose in the creation and evolution of the universe, long presumed by ancient faith and now confirmed by modern cosmology. And we can glimpse a larger purpose in the continuous operation of all that we can observe by consistent laws that are understandable to us. The conflation of faith and reason may not yet be a comfortable marriage, but at least proponents of each now agree that we are an integral part of something far larger than ourselves. And assumptions derived from both can now be proposed and considered without a sense of condescension.

Altruism may seem the more noble pole of our ethical compass, but taken by itself altruism leads us as far astray as unrestrained self-interest. The so-called "radical environmentalists" fall into this error. They quixotically reject human-caused environmental alteration while ignoring the natural role of self-interest in the interactions of all living things, humans included, with one another and with their environments. Simply put, whatever our motives, our activities are beneficial to some species and detrimental to others and have an effect upon the planet. On the other hand, we possess the power to exert some level of control over many, if not most, of these effects through our ethical choices.

In the real world of political infighting for conflicting fisheries management goals, or for that matter any resource management goals, self-interest is the crux, the north-pointing pole of our ethical compass, since altruism, unlike self-interest, is an insufficient source of motivation for most people. Self-interest is what ultimately must be appealed to if a "third-step" ethic is to be widely accepted and successfully applied to the task of restoring and maintaining ocean resources and of preserving Wilson's "world in which the human spirit was born."

More than a half-century ago, Aldo Leopold understood the interlocking nature of altruism and self-interest in ethics. He had also come to understand that an ethic that related man to his planet would require practical knowledge of how the relationship works. In *A Sand County Almanac*, he wrote:

> All ethics so far evolved rest upon a single premise: that the individual is a member of a community of interdependent parts. His instincts prompt him to compete for his place in that community, but his ethics prompt him also to cooperate (perhaps in order that there may be a place to compete for).

The key to a successful third-step ethic that allows us to use and benefit from our ocean resources—in fact, any of the renewable natural resources—while not depleting them is to truly know the interdependent parts. Therein lies the highest possible value of good science.

Knowledge is of little practical importance unless it is shared, however. The conclusions of our best science must be widely available, freely accessible, and easily understandable. You may be on the side of the angels, but your small contribution to conserving our most precious of birthrights is of little use if the forces of immorality and destruction are able to overwhelm your efforts through an appeal to ignorance. We must all be teachers and activists and even missionaries, although we must always guard against the arrogance of false certitude that ruins the efforts of many present-day environmentalists and even of some conservation organizations. It is important to be right, but it is essential also to win.

Competing self-interests can be complex, and human motivation is changeable, but wherever one's individual self-interests lie or whatever the source of one's particular motivation, an ethical compass based upon shared assumptions leads generally to the same place. A younger fisherman whose self-interest is building his business makes ethical choices that are similar to those of an older one whose self-interest is making certain that his grandchildren are able to experience the sea as he has. An ethical compass based upon our six assumptions, supported by adequate fisheries science, would have pointed toward different decisions that could have constrained the resource-destructive and ultimately self-destructive conduct of our fisheries that has occurred over the past three decades.

· · ·

This book is dedicated to my grandchildren, and there is really no secret why. My life can continue only through them, and I love them with a force that is stronger than the force of my own existence. The world of my childhood is gone forever. It was a good world, filled with freedom and optimism, but one my grandchildren can never really know.

I want to tell my grandchildren about the icy shock of diving into clear ocean water, the illicit joy of making love on a beach under a soft summer moon, the wild danger of a storm at sea, the loneliness of a fog-shrouded lighthouse with the gong of a bell buoy in the distance, the snap of sails on a broad reach in a stiff breeze, the taste of salt on the skin of a loved one, the smell of fresh seafood with beer and laughter among friends, the tears of walking on a cold winter beach after a staggering loss, the silent wonder at teeming life, the dark fear of the infinite beyond their own lives.

It is not necessary that they follow my path, but only that they have the kind of world in which they can follow their own, and this is what worries me. I want them to know the thrill of taking a chance on a risky venture and to have to fight and even to suffer to pass on to their grandchildren, to quote Wilson, "access to the world in which the human spirit was born."

For the sea and our lives are intertwined, and we are a part of its eternal life. The preservationist who would deny us our proper role in the life of the sea is as devoid of soul as the environmental rapist who would industrialize it. We function in the sea's ecosystem as predators, but that position must not provide us an excuse to be its destroyers. I want my grandchildren to know these things, and in truth, that is why I wrote this book.

BIBLIOGRAPHY

Benchley, Peter. *Jaws.* 1974

Berlin, Sven. *Jonah's Dream: A Meditation on Fishing.* 1964

Bigelow, Henry B., and William C. Schroeder. *Fishes of the Gulf of Maine.* 1953

Boeri, David, and James Gibson. *Tell It Good-Bye, Kiddo: The Decline of the New England Offshore Fishery.* 1976

Farrington, S. Kip, Jr., *Fishing the Atlantic, Offshore and On.* 1949

Frost, Robert, *The Poems of Robert Frost.* 1946

Grey, Zane. *Tales of Swordfish and Tuna.* 1927

Hemingway, Ernest. *On the Blue Water.* 1936

Hersey, John. *Blues.* 1987

Huxley, Thomas H. *Collected Essays.* 1893–94

Junger, Sebastian. *The Perfect Storm: A True Story of Men against the Sea.* 1997

Lang, Andrew. *Angling Sketches.* 1890

Leopold, Aldo. *A Sand County Almanac, with Essays on Conservation from Round River.* 1949

Lorenz, Konrad. *King Solomon's Ring.* 1952

Lyman, Henry, and Frank Woolner. *Complete Book of Striped Bass Fishing.* 1954

——*Striped Bass Fishing.* 1983

Margulis, Lynn. *Symbiotic Planet.* 1998

Melville, Herman. *Moby Dick.* 1851

Morison, Samuel Eliot. *The Great Explorers: The European Discovery of America.* 1978

National Marine Fisheries Service. "Fishery Management Plan for the Atlantic Bluefish." *Status of the Fishery Resources off the Northeastern United States.* 1987

National Research Council. *An Assessment of Atlantic Bluefin Tuna.* 1994

Preble, Dave, and Carl Safina. "A Rising Tide for Ethics." Paper presented at Yale University, New Haven, Connecticut, 2000

Reiger, George. *Profiles in Saltwater Angling.* 1973

——*The Striped Bass Chronicles.* 1997

Safina, Carl. *Song for the Blue Ocean.* 1997

Smith, Capt. John. *New England's Trials.* 1616

Steinbeck, John. *The Log from the* Sea of Cortez. 1941

Thoreau, Henry David. *Walden.* 1854

Verne, Jules. *Twenty Thousand Leagues under the Sea.* 1869

Walton, Izaak. *The Compleat Angler, or, The Contemplative Man's Recreation.* 1653

Williams, Ted. *Fishing to Win.* 1984

Wilson, Edward O. *The Diversity of Life.* 1992

Wood, William. *New England's Prospect.* 1634

Zern, Ed. *To Hell with Fishing.* 1945

INDEX